Better Homes and Gardens®

# Country Pleasures

## CHRISTMAS AT HOME

Better Homes and Gardens® Books

Des Moines, Iowa

Better Homes and Gardens®

# Country Pleasures

## CHRISTMAS AT HOME

*BETTER HOMES AND GARDENS® BOOKS, an imprint of Meredith® Books*
President, Book Group: Joseph J. Ward
Vice President, Editorial Director: Elizabeth P Rice

*For Better Homes and Gardens® Books*
Executive Editor: Maryanne Bannon
Senior Editor: Carol Spier
Associate Editor: Carolyn Mitchell
Production Manager: Bill Rose
Creative Editor: Joni Prittie
Creative Assistant: Ceci Powell
Food Editor: Joyce Trollope
Illustrations: Wade Rollins
Cover Photo: Julie Maris/Semel
Photographs and Styling: Joni Prittie,
except photos on pages 117, 122, 123, 140, 141, 153, 154, 155

*For Roundtable Press, Inc.*
Directors: Susan E. Meyer, Marsha Melnick
Executive Editor: Amy T. Jonak
Project Editor: Eleanor Levie
Copy Editor: Sue Heinemann
Design: Brian Sisco, Susan Evans, Sisco & Evans, New York
Design Associate: Betty Lew

ISBN: 0-696-02565-5 (hardcover)
ISBN: 0-696-20360-X (softcover)
ISSN: 1068-2910

Printed in the United States of America
10  9  8  7  6  5  4  3  2

**WE CARE!**

All of us at Better Homes and Gardens® Books are dedicated to offering you, our
customer, the best books we can create. We are particularly concerned that all of our
instructions for making projects are clear and accurate. Please address your correspon-
dence to Customer Service, Meredith Press, 150 East 52nd Street, New York, NY 10022.

Our seal assures you that every recipe in
*Christmas at Home:* COUNTRY PLEASURES
has been tested in the Better Homes and Gardens®
Test Kitchen. This means that every recipe is practical
and reliable, and meets our high standards of taste
appeal. We guarantee your satisfaction with this book
for as long as you own it.

If you would like to order additional copies of any of our books, call 1-800-678-2803
or check with your local bookstores.

# Country Pleasures

The simple joys of Christmas are what we treasure most. Family and friends. Sharing small pleasures and indulgences. We seek ways to put the "country" back in Christmas, somehow simplifying the hectic holiday season. ❖ The projects in this book are designed with simplicity in mind. They are easy; they require little special skill or equipment; and most can be made in an evening. Yet the results are wonderfully rewarding. ❖ With your own hands, you'll craft heartfelt gifts and homemade decorations your loved ones will treasure for years. And you'll find tasty recipes to flavor your holiday entertaining. ❖ We wish you a simply wonderful Christmas season filled with family, friends, fine food, and the joy of sharing gifts from the heart.

# CONTENTS

# Deck the Halls
## CELEBRATE & DECORATE

*Bring warmth, charm, and the most delightful accents to your home this season with decorations you make yourself. Within these pages, there's a new technique for everyone to try. Learn how easy it is to cut and punch metal, fuse appliqués in place, and bead ornaments.* ❖ *Want a real quick idea? Try the Homespun Wreath, no-sew Christmas Quilt, or Jingle Bell.* ❖ *For truly exquisite results destined to become family heirlooms, create the Ribbon-Weave Stocking, Cross-Stitch Kringle, and Glimmery Angel.* ❖ *Combine several techniques in the Father Christmas figure—a masterpiece that will have everyone oohing and aahing. Just don't tell them how easy it was!*

# Country COPPER AND TIN

*Try your hand at a craft that dates back to colonial America by cutting these 4"–6" ornaments from sheets of thin metal.*

**What You Will Need:**
8" × 10" sheet of copper
8" × 10" sheet of tin
22-gauge copper wire

*Items listed in How to Cut and Pierce Metal, page 11.*

**Prepare:** Read How to Cut and Pierce Metal, page 11.

**Cut Shapes:** Transfer patterns, then trace and cut out from metal, following directions in How to Cut and Pierce Metal. Trace small and large star patterns separately. Pierce holes for hanging as shown by open circles on pattern. Pierce decorative holes as desired.

**Hang:** Cut a 3" length of copper wire for each ornament. Thread wire through hole and twist ends together.

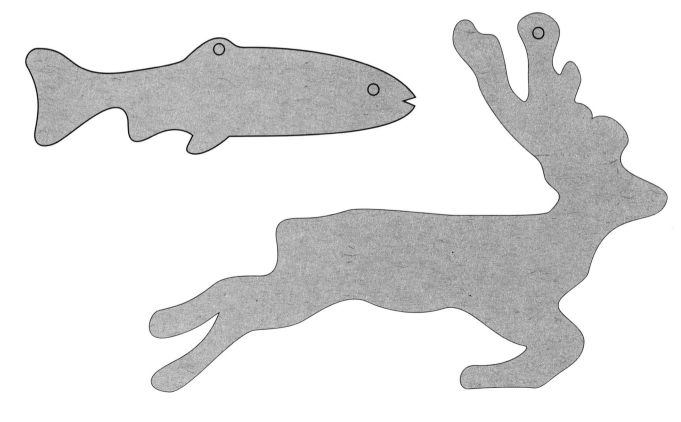

# Cut and Pierce Metal

❖ **What You Will Need:** 30-gauge metal sheets as indicated in project directions. These may be found in a local craft store, or contact Herrs & Acclaim (see Sources). You will also need tracing paper, soft lead pencil, old leather or cotton work gloves, tin snips or heavy scissors, thick piece of plywood or particleboard, rubber mallet, awl (or nails of varying sizes), and steel wool 0000.

❖ **Transfer Patterns:** Trace each actual-size pattern on tracing paper, or photocopy them; enlarge those which are not actual size with photocopier. Cut out patterns and tape onto metal sheets. Using awl or soft lead pencil, trace around pattern onto metal.

❖ **Cut Metal:** Wear gloves to protect hands from cuts and metal from fingerprints. You can use tin snips to cut out tin shapes, but a 5" pair of stainless-steel scissors works best. Use steel wool to smooth cut edges and clean surfaces.

❖ **Pierce Metal:** Place shapes on plywood or particle board. Tape edges of metal shapes to board. Using rubber mallet, pound shapes flat. Using mallet and awl, poke a hole for a hanger where shown on pattern by open circle. If desired, use awl to punch a design of dots or firmly mark a design line in metal.

ACTUAL-SIZE PATTERNS

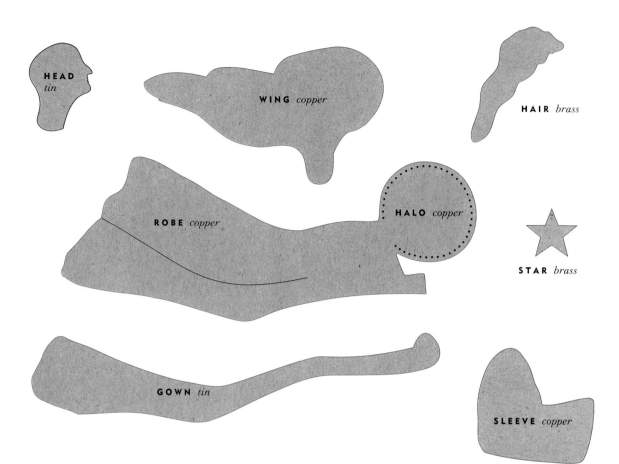

# *Glimmery* ANGEL

*Let this 9" long haloed and winged figure catch a falling star. Mix copper, tin, and brass for delicate contrasts.*

**What You Will Need:**

8" × 10" sheet of copper

8" × 10" sheet of tin

2" × 4" scrap of brass sheeting (optional)

22-gauge copper wire, 8" length

Soldering iron and solder

**Prepare:** Enlarge patterns by photocopying at 200%. Read How to Cut and Pierce Metal, on page 11. Cut out full-size patterns and transfer to metal sheets: robe/halo, wing, and sleeve to copper; head and gown to tin; star and hair to brass—or any available metal scrap.

**Cut shapes:** Place patterns on metal sheets and cut out pieces. Also cut out line on robe. Pound pieces flat, then clean with steel wool. Pierce holes around halo and on star with awl.

**Assemble Angel:** Following manufacturer's instructions for soldering iron, and referring to photo for position, solder pieces together in this order: gown and wing to robe, head to halo, add sleeve, then hair. Gently curve wire, insert one end through hole of star, and solder other end to back of hand. Insert thread through an enlarged hole in halo to make a hanging loop.

*Note: If your photocopier won't enlarge to 200%, enlarge image to 141%, and then enlarge resulting copy to 142%. To make a 400% enlargement, repeat process, starting with 200% copy.*

# CARD *Caddy*

*Wondering where to put all your colorful Christmas cards? Show them off in this decorative holiday basket, about 12" long.*

ACTUAL-SIZE
MOTIF

**What You Will Need:**

Slat-woven basket with handle, 12" long (this one in a diamond weave from Texas Baskets; see Sources)

Approximately 3½ yards pleated red ribbon, ⅜" wide

2½ yards green plaid ribbon, ⅞" wide

Green acrylic paint

Red acrylic paint in a squeeze bottle with tip

2 sprigs of artificial holly with berries

1 yard natural raffia

Paintbrushes

Scissors

Glue gun and glue sticks

Craft glue for beribboned slats

*Note: Read How to Use a Hot Glue Gun, page 47.*

**Paint Green Slats:** Paint handle, all surfaces of rim, and all slats slanted in one direction green. Allow paint to dry before proceeding.

**Create Ribboned Slats:** Cut two pieces of plaid ribbon, each twice the length of handle. Hot-glue one end of ribbon piece on slight diagonal to base of handle on the inside. Glue end of second ribbon over first, but slanted in opposite direction. Wrap ribbons around handle, crisscrossing them along entire length. Trim ends and hot-glue them to base of handle at opposite side. Cover every other row of unpainted slats with ribbon as follows: Hold green plaid ribbon against slat and cut a length to fit slat. Using a paintbrush, apply craft glue to reverse side of ribbon. Center ribbon on slat and press into place, tucking ends under painted slats. Wash paintbrush thoroughly in soapy water to remove glue.

**Add Holly Motif:** Using holly pattern as a guide, paint 3 holly leaves freehand on each remaining slat. Squeeze red paint to make a dot for each of 3 berries. Also use red paint to dot a berry between each crisscross of ribbon. Allow paint to dry completely.

**Finish:** Starting at bottom of rim, hot-glue red ribbon around rim in 3 overlapping layers. Also hot-glue red ribbon to underside of each edge of handle. Hot-glue sprigs of holly at each base of handle. Make 2 simple bows of raffia, each about 3½" wide. Tie a knot in each streamer end. Hot-glue a bow over center of each holly sprig.

# SEED BEAD *Heart*

*Show your heart with this 3" beaded ornament that sparkles with Christmas feeling.*

**What You Will Need:**

10" square of red felt

Size 11 seed beads, 1 package each: red transparent, white transparent, gold metallic

Size 12 beading needle

Size 0 beading thread

Tracing paper

Pencil

Straight pins

Small amount of polyester stuffing

Scissors

ACTUAL-SIZE PATTERN

**Create Heart:** Trace actual-size heart pattern onto tracing paper and cut out. Pin pattern to felt; cut out 2 heart shapes. Thread 30" of beading thread on needle, pull ends even, and knot. Hold heart shapes together. Make edge-lace stitches as follows, referring to diagrams. Take a stitch, starting at top center of hearts. Thread on a gold bead and repeat stitch through felt, returning through gold bead. String on 1 red, 1 white, 1 red, and 1 gold bead. Take a stitch through felt and come up through hole of last gold bead. Continue, repeating same pattern of beads and stitching only gold beads to felt. (Other beads are simply strung on thread between each gold bead.) Continue this pattern until 1½" from first bead. Place a small amount of batting into heart and continue beading pattern to close heart. Manipulate spacing in order to end

without disrupting pattern, and thread needle through first gold bead. To end off, stitch through hearts, back through same gold bead and next 4 beads and heart again before knotting. Trim thread.

**Bead Hanging Loop:** Thread 20" of beading thread on needle, pull ends even and knot. Take a stitch through center top of heart. String on 12 white beads and a pattern of 1 gold, 1 red, 1 white, 1 red, 1 gold. Add 10 white beads and repeat pattern. Add 4½" of white beads. Repeat pattern, add 10 white beads, repeat pattern, then add 12 white beads. Stitch through heart and fasten off securely. Trim thread ends.

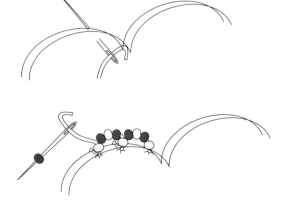

**DIAGRAMS**

# MINI *Stocking*

*Calling all needlepointers! This 4"-high folk-art stocking is ready to fill with tiny treasures.*

**What You Will Need:**
White needlepoint canvas, 10 mesh-to-the-inch
DMC tapestry yarn, Article 486: 1 skein each
  red #7138, green #7346, yellow #7726, ecru
*Equipment listed in How to Needlepoint, page 17.*

**Needlepoint:** Cut two 5" × 6" rectangles of canvas. Read How to Needlepoint, on page 17. Following general instructions, tape edges and work in continental stitch. Turn chart upside down and begin with a straight corner.

Work design on one piece of canvas, following chart. Work design on second piece of canvas, following chart in reverse, to produce a mirror image of the first.

**Assemble:** Trim canvas to within 3 rows of needle-work. Fold over top row and secure to back with a few stitches, taking care that they do not show through to right side. Fold under unstitched areas of canvas, leaving just 1 empty mesh all around. Place front on back, wrong sides together. To join edges, use green yarn and overcast-stitch along empty rows of mesh. Strive to follow diagonal direction of continental stitches. Leave top open.

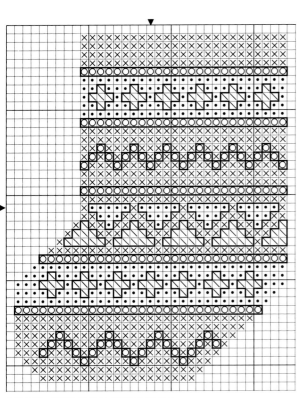

**CHART FOR MINI STOCKING**

**COLOR KEY**

☒ *Green*

◩ *Red*

⊡ *Ecru*

◯ *Yellow*

**Add Hanging Loop:** Cut 10" strands of yarn: 1 each from green, red and yellow yarns. Knot one end of all 3 strands together and secure temporarily to a hook on a wall. Holding strands at opposite end, twist them tightly. Hold twist at center, folding twisted yarn in half, and slide fingers through yarn up to hook. Yarn will kink up and maintain twist. Hold both ends together and knot, leaving a loop 2½" long. Trim away yarn past knot. Tack knot to inside of stocking at top, above heel.

For needlepoint projects in this book, you will be using tapestry yarn on white canvas, 10 mesh-to-the-inch. You will also need the following pieces of equipment: #20 tapestry needle, masking tape, and scissors.

❖ **Prepare Canvas:** Cut canvas to size indicated in individual project directions, then tape edges of canvas to prevent raveling. Begin at lower right corner of canvas, 1" from right and bottom edges.

❖ **Work Design:** Use 1 strand of yarn in needle throughout. Follow chart, which shows a symbol designating color of yarn for each stitch. Work design on canvas to correspond to the symbols on chart.

❖ **Stitch:** To begin any stitch, leave a short (1") tail on back and work over it. To end, insert needle under a few stitches on the back. Do not make knots.

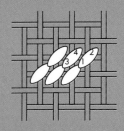

The most common needle-point stitch is the continental stitch. To start, bring needle up through canvas where indicated on stitch detail by number 1. Bring needle down at 2, up at 3, and down at 4. Proceed with this diagonal pattern for each symbol in the same color until you get to the end of the row. Turn work and chart upside down to work even rows from right to left also. Finish working all of symbols for first color, then proceed to second color and work all stitches for that color. Proceed in this manner until needlepoint is completed.

The overcast stitch is a simple diagonal stitch used to finish edges and join two pieces of needlepoint mesh together.

# *Christmas* QUILT

*Taking just one stitch for each red bow, you can quilt a joyful 25" square wall hanging. Tie it onto a twiggy hanger for a rustic look.*

**What You Will Need:**

2 yards of muslin fabric

½ yard red-and-white checked fabric

¼ yard green small-scale plaid fabric for trees

Small amounts of assorted cotton fabrics in green, white, and/or red

2 yards paper-backed fusible web

Roll fusible web tape, ½" wide

25" square of quilt batting

Small amount of red sport-weight yarn

Decorative twig hanger

Assorted Christmas buttons (shown here: 8 gingerbread men, 5 angels, 6 red rocking horses, 4 sleighs, 4 Santa bears, 4 gold stars, 3 Santas, 5 wreaths, 3 candles, 5 drums, 3 snowmen, 2 stockings, 3 Santa's heads, 4 Christmas trees)

Pencil

Ruler

Cardboard

Tracing paper

Scissors

Straight pins

Tapestry needle

Iron

Glue gun and glue sticks

*Note: Read How to Use a Hot Glue Gun, page 47.*

**Form Blocks:** Make a window template: Referring to the diagram below, cut a 5" square opening in the center of an 8" square piece of cardboard. Place this window template on right sides of fabrics and mark 5" squares with pencil; window opening allows you to center stripes either straight or diagonally. Mark 8 blocks on red check fabric and 8 blocks on assorted other green, white, or red fabrics. From fusible web, cut out sixteen 6" squares. Following manufacturer's directions, fuse to wrong sides of marked squares. Cut out backed squares along marked lines. You should have sixteen 5" square blocks.

**Make Trees:** Apply fusible web to back of green plaid fabric. Using the actual-size pattern on page 20, cut a tree window template out of a 5"×6" piece of cardboard. Place the window on plaid with stripes centered vertically, and mark around the tree form with pencil. Cut out. Repeat to mark and cut 8 trees. Peel off paper backing and center a tree on each red check fabric block. Iron to fuse into place.

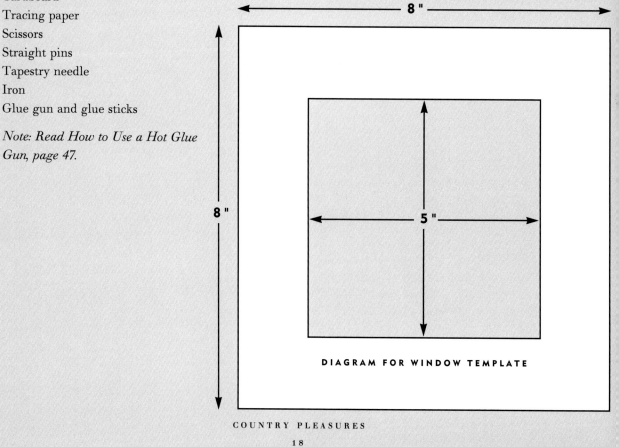

**DIAGRAM FOR WINDOW TEMPLATE**

ACTUAL-SIZE PATTERN FOR TREE TEMPLATE

**Prepare Quilt Top:** From muslin, cut two 26" squares. On one (front), press edges ½" to wrong side all around. On the other (back), press edges ⅝" to wrong side all around. Working on a flat surface, arrange squares on right side of front: refer to photo for suggested arrangement, and leave 1" between blocks and outer edges. Working on one block at a time, carefully peel off backing and iron to fuse into place.

**Assemble:** Turn quilt front wrong side up and unfold edges. Lay quilt batting on top, then fold edges over batting. Secure with pins. Pin quilt back, centered, on top of batting. Pin fusible web tape under all edges and iron to fuse.

**Tie Quilt:** Tie quilt muslin layers together through center of each intersection of blocks as follows: Thread 10" of yarn onto tapestry needle. Bring needle from front to back of quilt, then back up to front, a scant ⅛" away. Tie ends in a simple bow and trim ends even. Using a doubled 18" length of yarn, tie quilt at top corners to twig hanger. Tie bow at top ends of yarn.

**Add Ornaments:** Using hot glue, attach buttons to fabric trees as ornaments. (Here, a gingerbread man was glued beside each tree.)

# Teddy Bear TREE SKIRT

*Invite jolly teddy bears and candy canes to dance around your tree on this 55"-diameter tree skirt that requires no sewing at all.*

**What You Will Need:**

Ready-made red felt tree skirt, 55" in diameter

1 yard cotton fabric featuring large-scale print of teddy bears and candy canes or any other Christmas images

5 yards cotton cording, ½" in diameter

1 yard paper-backed fusible web

Scissors

Iron

Glue gun and glue sticks

*Note: Read How to Use a Hot Glue Gun, page 47.*

**Prepare Shapes:** Following manufacturer's instructions, apply fusible web to back of Christmas print fabric. Cut out teddy bears, candy canes, assorted holly berry patterns, or any other desired motifs. Peel off paper backing and arrange shapes around tree skirt to decorate, referring to photo. Iron to fuse in place.

**Finish:** Using hot glue, adhere cotton cording around outside edge of skirt. Trim excess.

# *Teddy Angel* STOCKING

*With this 17"-high angelic charmer, your mantel will twinkle with holiday cheer.*

**What You Will Need:**

½ yard each green and white felt

¼ yard bear angel fabric

¾ yard candy-striped ribbon or trim from fabric

¼ yard paper-backed fusible web

Set of battery-powered miniature Christmas lights such as Flora-Lite Co's product (see Sources)

Green thread

Straight pins

Scissors

Iron

Sewing needle or sewing machine

Craft knife #1

Masking tape

**Cut Stocking Pieces:** Enlarge stocking pattern at right to 400% by photocopying at 200% twice. Pin actual-size stocking pattern to green felt, and cut out 2 pieces.

**Prepare Iron-ons:** Following manufacturer's instructions, apply squares of fusible web to back of 5 bears on fabric and to back of white felt. Cut out bears and set aside. Cut out four 2½" squares and one 3¼" square from white felt. Fold each square in half twice to form a smaller square. With scissors, cut felt as shown in diagram or as desired to make snowflakes. Peel paper backing off bears and snowflakes, and place on the front of one stocking piece, adhesive side down and referring to photo for suggested arrangement. Iron to fuse.

**Set Up Lights:** Use tip of craft knife to make small holes in stocking where twinkle lights will be placed (position battery pack at stocking toe). Force bulbs through from the back. Use masking tape to hold wires and battery pack in place, at least ½" from stocking edges.

**Assemble:** With right sides together, pin stocking front to back. Stitch around all but top edge, using ¼" seam allowances. Clip curves and turn right side out, being sure that all lights remain securely taped in position. Position battery pack inside stocking toe. For cuff, cut 16" × 8" piece of white

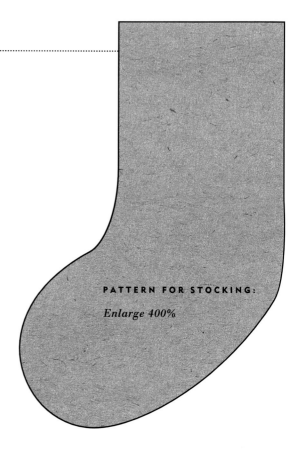

**PATTERN FOR STOCKING:**

*Enlarge 400%*

felt. Fold crosswise in half, and stitch along short ends, forming a tube. Fold the tube in half, right side out, aligning raw edges. Pin raw edges of cuff to top of stocking, aligning seam at heel. Stitch pieces together, ½" from edges. Fold cuff over stocking. Cut 16" of candy-striped trim and pin along right side of cuff, ¾" from fold. Topstich trim. For a hanging loop, cut 11" strip of ribbon or trim. Turn under ¼" on each side, press, and secure with running stitches. Stitch edges inside cuff above heel.

*Note: If your photocopier won't enlarge to 200%, enlarge image to 141%, and then enlarge resulting copy to 142%. To make a 400% enlargement, repeat process, starting with 200% copy.*

**DIAGRAM FOR SNOWFLAKE**

# Ribbon Weave STOCKING

*Surprise Santa with a festive 17"-long stocking, enlivened with a rich surface texture created by an easy weaving technique. Vary the look with your choice of ribbons.*

## What You Will Need:

1½ yards red felt

⅛ yard white felt

Gold-dot, gold-edge wired ribbon, 1⅝" wide:
  4½ yards green, 3 yards red

½ yard paper-backed fusible web

Motif from Christmas fabric with bear, angel,
  or other print

½ yard cotton cording, ¼" in diameter

Red, green, and white thread

Straight pins

Scissors

Iron

Sewing machine with zipper foot

**Cut Stocking Pieces:** Enlarge stocking pattern on page 19 to 400% by photocopying at 200% twice, or until stocking measures 17" in length. Pin actual-size pattern on fabrics: cut 2 from red felt and 1 from fusible web.

**Weave Ribbon:** Following manufacturer's instructions, iron fusible web to one felt stocking piece (stocking front). Peel off paper backing and place on flat surface. Align one 14" length of green gold-dot ribbon along long edge of stocking at heel side. Pin at top. Lay subsequent strands down entire length of stocking, cutting ribbon to lengths necessary to cover stocking front as you go.

Arrange so that ribbon edges are butting and parallel, and pin at top edges. See Diagram 1. Lay strips of red gold-dot ribbon crosswise, so that they cover stocking and green ribbon strips. Pin in place along both ends of each ribbon. See Diagram 2. Beginning at top, unpin one end of each red ribbon and weave it under and over green ribbons. Alternate the weaving pattern to obtain a checkerboard pattern. See Diagram 3. Repin the ribbons as they are woven in. When weaving is complete, iron to fuse.

**Assemble:** For cuff, cut four 4½" × 8" rectangles from white felt. Pin 1 to top edge of each stocking piece with right sides together and stitch across, ¼" from top edge. Make covered cord: Lay cotton cording along wrong side of green ribbon, and bring ribbon edges together. Using a zipper foot to get as close as possible to cording, stitch along ribbon. Cut covered cord in half and pin to one long edge of each remaining white felt rectangle. With cording in between, and aligning raw edges, pin felt rectangles to top of stocking; stitch.

Pin stocking pieces with right sides together and cuffs extended. Stitch around all but top edges, using ¼" seam allowance. Clip curves and turn stocking right side out; fold cuff so that covered cord is at top, and stitch remaining edge of white felt cuff to inside of stocking. Fold cuff down over stocking.

Iron paper-backed fusible web to back of fabric featuring bear, angel, sprig of holly, or other desired motif. Cut out motif(s), peel off paper backing, and referring to photo, position on cuff. Iron to fuse, using a pressing cloth to protect white felt.

For a hanging loop, fold remaining red ribbon in half lengthwise and crosswise; stitch short ends inside the cuff above heel.

*Note: If your photocopier won't enlarge to 200%, enlarge image to 141%, and then enlarge resulting copy to 142%. To make a 400% enlargement, repeat process, starting with 200% copy.*

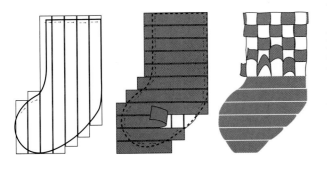

DIAGRAM 1        DIAGRAM 2        DIAGRAM 3

# *Homespun* WREATH

*Bring nostalgic charm to a wreath (8" or 10" in diameter) with colonial-style fabrics and evocative scents of pine, spices, and apple.*

**What You Will Need:**

⅛ yard each of 3 different homespun-style fabrics

1 yard medium-weight wire (22–24 gauge)

⅝ yard burgundy-check craft ribbon 1" wide

Thread to match fabrics

Small amount of high-loft quilt batting

Christmas potpourri (optional)

Twine

Sewing needle or sewing machine

Scissors

Pinking shears

Wire cutters

**Create "Sausages":** Using pinking shears, cut out 5" squares: 3 from each fabric for large wreath, 2 from each fabric for small wreath. Fold each square in half, wrong side out. Sew along long edges, using ¼" seam allowances. Turn each tube right side out. From batting, cut a 3½" square for each tube. Roll and push into center of tube. (If desired, insert a pinch of potpourri in center.) Thread wire through center of each stuffed tube, alternating fabrics. After sliding onto wire, tightly wrap and tie ends of each tube close to batting with 5" pieces of twine. When all sausages are on wire, bring wire ends together to form a ring and twist to secure; clip excess wire.

**Finish:** Tie a simple ribbon bow to top of wreath. For a hanging loop, tie on 8" length of twine.

# *Jingle* BELL

*Ring in the holidays with this 3"-high stuffed ornament.*
*Make in a jiffy—one for your own tree or dozens for*
*Christmas bazaars.*

**What You Will Need:**

4" × 7" rectangle of cotton fabric

¼ yard red or green grosgrain ribbon, ⅛" wide

1 yard gold-and-red passementerie trim

½ yard gold-and-green passementerie trim

Thread to match fabric

Red embroidery floss

Small jingle bell

Small amount of polyester stuffing

Tracing paper

Pencil

Straight pins

Sewing needle or sewing machine

Embroidery needle

Glue gun and glue sticks (optional)

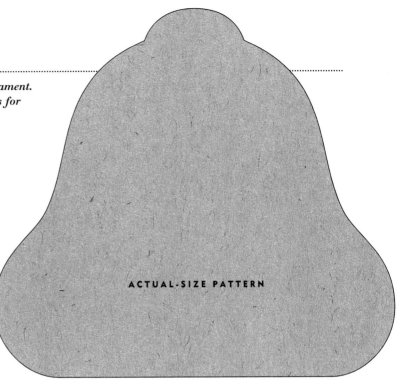

ACTUAL-SIZE PATTERN

**Create Basic Shape:** Trace actual-size pattern and use to cut 2 bell shapes from fabric. Pin shapes with right sides together and stitch around, using a ¼" seam allowance, leaving a 2" opening at top. Clip corners and curves; turn right side out. Stuff plumply. Slip-stitch opening closed, catching the ends of grosgrain ribbon at top, for hanging loop.

**Add Trim:** Read How to Use a Hot Glue Gun, on page 47. Tack or hot-glue trim to the ornament: Beginning at a seam, apply horizontal, vertical, or diagonal rows of trim on both sides of ornament. Beginning and ending at top, apply trim along seams. Finally, wrap trim around hanging loop.

Using embroidery needle and floss, attach jingle bell at center bottom.

# CROSS-STITCH *Bells*

*Give family members' pictures a ringing endorsement inside these embroidered frames. Hang the 3½" × 4½" bells as ornaments, or display them on easel stands.*

**What You Will Need For Each Bell:**

3½" × 4½" bell-shaped self-stick Christmas ornament forms (available from Pres-On Merchandising Corp.; see Sources)

7" square of 14-count even-weave fabric (here, Charles Craft Reserve in Platinum [pale gray], Aspen [sage], and Linaida [beige])

1–2 holiday pipe cleaners for hanging ornament

Favorite family photo to fit window opening

Felt or Christmas wrapping paper for backing (optional)

Additional pipe cleaners or trim to embellish edges

1 skein embroidery floss in each color listed in color key

Rainbow Glissen Gloss (see color chart)

Tacky glue

Glue gun and glue sticks

*Equipment listed in How to Cross-Stitch, page 30*

**Embroider:** Read How to Cross-Stitch, on page 30. Follow directions to prepare fabric and make cross-stitches, but use 1 Glissen thread along with 2 strands of floss.

On bird design, after cross-stitching is completed, follow chart to outline doves in backstitch using 1 strand of DMC #413. Use DMC #310 to make a French knot for partridge eye as shown by dot on stitching chart.

**Assemble:** To mount embroidered fabric on bell shape, carefully follow manufacturer's instructions included with the self-stick ornament. Be sure to center designs on ornament form. Position photo in portrait area of frame; center; and trim to fit. Set aside.

Read How to Use a Hot Glue Gun, on page 47. Trace backing piece of bell shape onto wrapping paper or felt. Cut out and secure in place with tacky glue. Align backing piece and front piece; bond with hot glue. Also hot-glue pipe cleaners or trim around bell edges. Trim excess. To hang ornament, bring ends of 2 pipe cleaners together and twist; hot-glue ends to back of ornament.

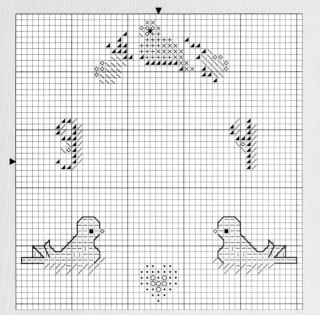

**BIRDS DESIGN**

## BIRDS COLOR KEY

| Floss | Metallic Thread |
|---|---|
| ◪ Emerald | Emerald Green |
| ⊠ Dark Brown | Copper |
| ⊞ Light Brown | Copper |
| ◩ Yellow | Soft Gold |
| ◇ Tan | Copper |
| ◰ Moss Green | Emerald Green |
| ⊟ Light Gray | Silver |
| ⊡ Medium Gray | Silver |
| • Cranberry | Red |
| ◯ Bright Red | Red |
| ■ Black | |

## RIBBON COLOR KEY

| Floss | Metallic Thread |
|---|---|
| ◕ Cherry Red | Red |
| ✳ Rust | Brick Red |
| ⊟ Apricot | Iridescent Apricot |
| ◇ Bright Yellow | Soft Gold |
| ▷ Light Green | Lime Green |
| ◣ Dark Green | Emerald Green |
| ♡ Red | Red |

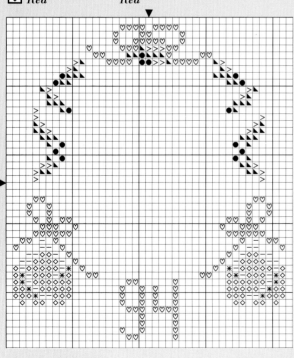

**RIBBON DESIGN**

## HOLLY COLOR KEY

| Floss | Metallic Thread |
|---|---|
| ◤ Dark Green | Emerald Green |
| ◿ Moss Green | Lime Green |
| • Cranberry | Red |
| ◯ Bright Red | Red |
| ▽ Light Blue | Iridescent Pale Blue |
| ▼ Dark Blue | Iridescent Blue |

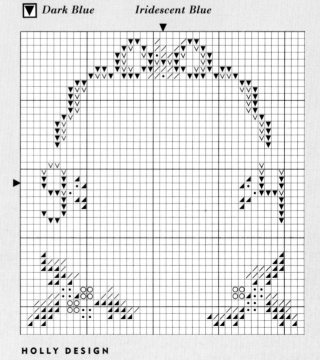

**HOLLY DESIGN**

# HOW TO
# *Cross-Stitch*

**Materials You Will Need:** Even-weave fabric as indicated in individual project directions, 6-strand embroidery floss in colors indicated.

**Equipment You Will Need:** #24 tapestry needle, scissors, small embroidery hoop (optional), straight pins, masking tape or zigzag sewing machine.

**Prepare Fabrics:** Prewash all-cotton fabrics, including even-weave fabrics, to preshrink them; let dry, then press. Cut even-weave fabric along the grain or as indicated. Tape or zigzag-stitch edges to prevent raveling. Fold each fabric piece in half vertically and horizontally to locate center; mark intersecting threads with a pin. For optimum results, place fabric in embroidery hoop to keep fabric taut; move hoop as needed.

**Get Started:** Cut floss into 18" lengths. To begin a strand, leave an end on back and work over it to secure; to end, run needle under 4 or 5 stitches on back of work. See Diagram 1. Following individual chart and color key, stitch each design with 2 strands of floss (each strand separated from 6-strand skein)

DIAGRAM 1

in needle, beginning at pin with stitch indicated by arrows on chart. If arrows point to a blank area, count squares to nearest symbol, then count threads to arrive at corresponding intersection of threads on even-weave fabric, and start there. Each symbol on chart represents 1 cross-stitch worked over the intersection of 1 horizontal and 1 vertical fabric thread (or set of threads); different symbols represent different colors.

**Make Cross-Stitches:** A single cross-stitch is formed in 2 motions. Following the numbering in Diagram 2, bring

DIAGRAM 2

threaded needle up at 1, down at 2, up at 3, down at 4, completing the stitch. Make crosses touch by inserting needle in same hole used for adjacent stitch. Work horizontal rows of stitches whenever possible.

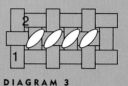

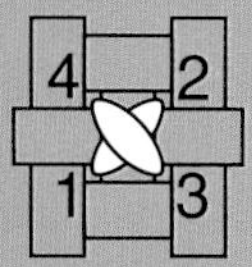

DIAGRAM 3

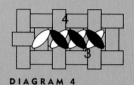

DIAGRAM 4

Referring to Diagram 3, bring thread up at 1 and down at 2; repeat to end of row in same color floss, forming first half of each stitch. Complete the stitches, 3–4, 3–4, on the return journey right to left; see Diagram 4. When a vertical row of stitches is appropriate, complete each stitch, then proceed to the next. No matter how you work the stitches, make sure that all crosses slant in the same direction: Work all underneath stitches in one direction and all top stitches in the opposite direction. Also make sure all strands lie smooth and flat: allow needle to hang freely from work occasionally to untwist floss.

## How to Backstitch
Dark lines on the cross-stitch chart indicate backstitching. Backstitch with a single strand of contrasting floss to define details. See Diagram 5.

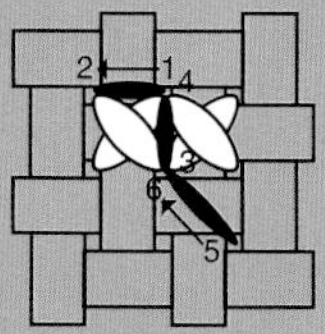

## How to Make a French Knot
French knots are shown on cross-stitch charts by black dots that do not fit

DIAGRAM 5

neatly within a square of the grid. To make a French knot, bring needle to right side of fabric where you wish knot to be. Holding the floss tautly with your other hand, twist floss twice around the needle. See Diagram 6. Insert needle back through fabric 1 or 2 fine threads away from where it emerged; keep holding floss tautly as you pull needle through. See Diagram 7.

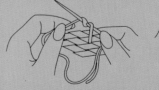

DIAGRAM 6

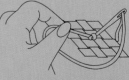

DIAGRAM 7

# CROSS-STITCH
# *Snowflakes*

*Conjure up thoughts of a wintry forest by stuffing these lovely 1"–3" ornaments with a little pine or balsam potpourri.*

**What You Will Need:**

Three 5" squares of 18-count navy Aida cloth

Three 5" squares of 14-count light oatmeal Fiddler's cloth

6-strand embroidery floss: 1 skein each white and light blue (DMC #793)

Small amounts of muslin and navy blue cotton fabrics for backing

1 yard fine pearl trim

1 yard narrow silver rickrack

Sewing thread to match trims

Polyester stuffing

Potpourri (optional)

Sewing needle or sewing machine

*Equipment listed in How to Cross-Stitch, page 30*

**Embroider:** Read How to Cross-Stitch, page 30. Follow directions to prepare fabric and work cross-stitches. Refer to photos and use a contrasting color floss for each even-weave fabric. Following chart for selected snowflake pattern, begin at center and work outward.

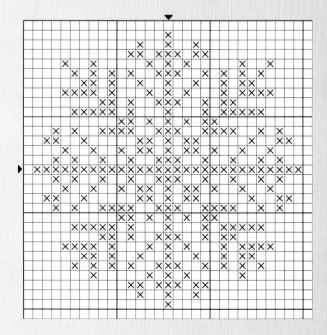

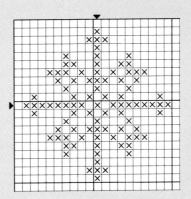

**Assemble:** After pattern is completed, cut even-weave fabric to desired size and shape around snowflake, leaving at least ½" all around embroidery. Cut backing fabric to same size. Pin embroidered fabric to backing with right sides together. Machine- or hand-stitch around, using ¼" seam allowances, leaving a 1" opening on one side. Turn ornament right side out and stuff to desired fullness with polyester stuffing, potpourri, or both. Slip-stitch opening closed.

**Finish:** Tack trim along seam all around edges of ornament; at top center, leave a loop with which to hang ornament.

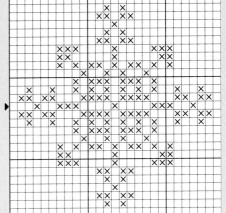

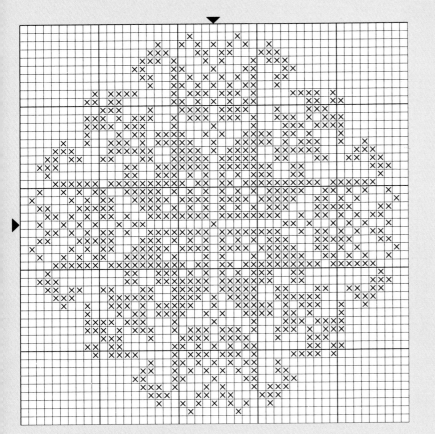

# CROSS-STITCH *Kringle*

*Picture Santa in a 9" frame or on a 15" pillow, spreading holiday cheer year after year.*

**What You Will Need:**

15" square of Zweigart Hearthside 14-count fabric with red or green border

6-strand embroidery floss: 1 skein each color listed in color key

Tapestry needle #24

Small red jingle bell

Tiny gold bead as tree topper

9 silver seed beads

14–18 green, gold, and silver seed beads for tree ornaments

Beading needle

Beading thread

*Equipment listed in How to Cross-Stitch, page 30*

*For Frame*:

Square frame as desired

Foam board to fit frame

Square of quilt batting to fit foam board

*For Pillow*:

1½ yards natural flat crocheted trim, ⅜" wide

15" square pillow form

½ yard dark green print cotton fabric

Thread to match fabric

Sewing needle and pins

Sewing machine

**Embroider:** Read How to Cross-Stitch, page 30. Follow directions to prepare fabric and cross-stitch. After cross-stitching is completed, follow chart to outline shapes in backstitch using 1 strand of floss: #535 for both sides of beard and hair; #814 for hat, outer edge of robe and

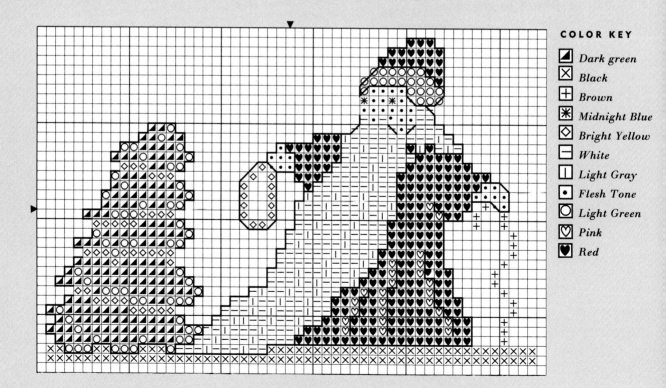

**COLOR KEY**

◩ Dark green
☒ Black
⊞ Brown
✳ Midnight Blue
◇ Bright Yellow
⊟ White
◫ Light Gray
• Flesh Tone
○ Light Green
♡ Pink
♥ Red

creases in robe; #810 for hands; #367 for tree; and #742 for garland.

**Add Beads:** Using beading thread and needle, secure red bell to top of cap and gold bead to top of tree. Add silver beads to beard, and gold, green, and silver beads to tree as ornaments.

**Make Frame:** Cover 14" board in quilt batting, then center embroidery on top. Stretch edges taut to wrong side of board and tape. Mount in frame without glass.

**Make Pillow:** Cut two 18" squares from dark green fabric. Center embroidery on one square (pillow front). Pin in place. Machine-stitch flat trim to raw edges of embroidered panel, securing it to pillow front. Pin pillow front to remaining fabric square (back) with right sides together. Machine-stitch along 3 sides, using ½" seam allowances. Clip corners and turn right side out. Slip square pillow form inside and hand-stitch opening closed.

# FATHER *Christmas*

*Standing 12" tall, this jovial Santa centerpiece is both fun to look at and fun to make.*

**What You Will Need:**

Round wood disk 8" in diameter, for base

4 ounces clay designed to be oven-baked

½ yard red felt, 60" wide

½" × 13" strip of brown felt, leather, or vinyl, for belt

11" × 26" piece of brown fabric, for cape

½" strips of fake fur, for trim

8" × 12" piece of check fabric, for sack

Twig, 10" long, for staff

13" length of wool roving, for hair and beard

1 yard medium-gauge wire

Green, red, tan, and peach acrylic paints

Clear acrylic spray, satin finish

24" strand of worsted-weight dark green yarn

Scraps of terry cloth

Empty, clean, 22-oz. detergent bottle

Small amount of polyester stuffing

Small amount of quilt batting

Tiny belt buckle

3 tiny jingle bells

Assorted miniature toys, ornaments, pinecones, and packages, to spill out of sack

Paintbrushes: 1" flat, #2 fan, #1 0/0 detail

Clay-sculpting tools

Sandpaper

Baking sheet

Aluminum foil

Blush make-up and sponge-tip applicator

Pencil

Embroidery and sewing needles

Ruler or tape measure

Red thread

Scissors

Glue gun and glue sticks

*Note: Read How to Use a Hot Glue Gun, page 47.*

**Prepare Base:** Using sandpaper, sand round wood disk until smooth. Brush off all wood dust. Using flat brush and green paint, paint entire base green. Allow paint to dry before proceeding. Moisten a piece of terry cloth with clean water and dip into tan paint. Work into green base to give a slightly antique look. Wipe dry with clean piece of terry cloth and allow to dry.

**Set Up Foundation:** Hot-glue detergent bottle on base toward back, to allow room for toy bag. (Hot glue will melt bottom of bottle, but it will nonetheless fuse the bottle to the base.) Add thick line of glue around bottom of bottle to further stabilize. Make ball of fiberfill about 4" in diameter. Hot-glue ball against center of bottle to form stomach (see Diagram 1). Cut 7" × 12" rectangle of quilt batting. Wrap around stomach and bottle, placing edges at back and using hot glue to secure.

**DIAGRAM 1**

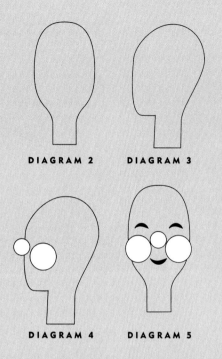

**DIAGRAM 2**  **DIAGRAM 3**

**DIAGRAM 4**  **DIAGRAM 5**

**Create Face:** Divide clay into one 3-ounce ball and one 1-ounce ball. Pull small piece off 3-ounce ball of clay and set aside for nose and cheeks. Shape rest of large piece into light-bulb form, pulling neck from bottom that will fit inside bottle neck. See Diagram 2. Pull out and shape chin (Diagram 3). Add round ball from extra piece for nose, and two other balls for cheeks (Diagram 4). Using sculpture tools, blend edges of balls into face. Referring to Diagram 5, make two half-moon indentations above cheeks for Santa's closed, smiling eyes. Make half-moon indentation below nose for his mouth. Shape bottom lip, and use pencil to make nostrils in nose. Use tools and fingers to get expression and shape you desire. Using needle, make little creases and laugh lines around, over, and under Santa's eyes.

**ACTUAL-SIZE PATTERN**

**Fashion Arms:** For mittens, divide remaining 1-ounce piece of clay into 2 pieces. Place over actual-size mitten pattern and shape. Smooth edges. Cut 36" length of wire to form arms. Double wire and twist ends together

in center (see Diagram 6). Twist wire together until it forms one piece with ends rounded and flattened. Insert mitten onto each rounded end. Shape mittens so one will curl around staff and the other curves around sack of toys.

**Bake:** Line baking sheet with foil. Place head and arms on sheet and bake following manufacturer's instructions for clay. Remove from oven and let cool completely.

**Assemble:** Apply hot glue to neck of Santa's head and insert into neck of bottle. Apply extra glue around bottle neck to seal. When glue is dry, apply peach paint to head using fan brush. Let paint dry. Paint mittens green; let dry. Brush a coat of tan paint over all clay items, filling in all

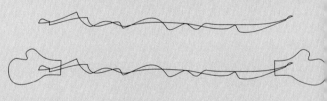

**DIAGRAM 6**

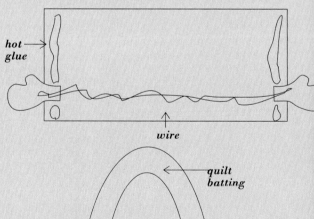

hot glue

wire

quilt batting

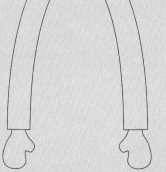

**DIAGRAM 7**

wrinkles and creases. Wipe off excess paint with clean, damp piece of terry cloth. When skin tone is as desired, allow paint to dry completely. Use detail brush and red paint to define lower lip. Apply blusher with sponge-tip applicator to cheeks. Measure length of arms from mitten to mitten. From quilt batting, cut a 5½"-wide rectangle to this length. Wrap batting around wire, hot-gluing along edges to secure. (See Diagram 7.)

**Make Clothing:** Trace actual-size patterns on next page. Tape sections of cape and robe together to complete half patterns; place these patterns on fabric folded in half, with long dash lines along fold. Use patterns to cut 1 robe and 1 hat from red felt. Also from red felt, cut out a 5½" × 13¼" rectangle, for sleeves. Use pattern to cut cape from brown fabric; set this aside. Fold robe in half with wrong sides together, and sew seam on red felt as indicated by short-dash (sewing) lines. Repeat with hat; clip across seam allowance at peak. Fold sleeve lengthwise in half and stitch along long edges. Turn all pieces right side out. Slip robe over head with seam at center back. Secure in place with hot glue inside neckline. To make belt, attach buckle to one end of the strip of leather, vinyl, or felt. Wrap belt around figure with buckle centered in front, securing in place with hot glue. Insert padded arms into sleeve, securing batting to felt inside wrists with dots of hot glue. Bend arms into U-shape and apply hot

glue generously at center. See Diagram 8. Gently wrap arms around back at the shoulder area. Hold in place until glue has cooled and set. Secure cape around shoulders with hot glue.

**Add Hair:** Pull a 3" length of wool roving to use as eyebrows and mustache and set aside. For hair, cut 9" length of wool roving. Draw line of hot glue from forehead to nape down center of head.. Press center of wool securely into glue and allow to dry. Arrange hair around face, securing in place with hot glue where necessary. Butt ends of roving at back and glue from underneath. Place remaining wool roving onto beard pattern and trim to shape. Place dots of hot glue around mouth and chin and carefully press roving into place. Secure to chin with additional hot glue. For eyebrows and mustache, twist small pieces of roving and secure to face with tiny dots of glue. Trim ends to a point.

**Put On Hat:** To attach hat, line bottom edge with hot glue and secure to top of head. Hot-glue strip of fake fur around bottom, trimming ends so they butt at back. Fold hat point to one side, secure in position with hot glue, and attach a small ball of fake fur or jingle bells at tip.

**Finish:** Using hot glue, secure red felt robe to base, draping and folding as needed. Attach fake fur strip around bottom of robe and to base. Overlap at back and trim. Measure around cuffs and cut two strips of fur to these lengths. Secure around cuffs with hot glue.

**Add sack:** Fold check fabric crosswise in half, wrong side out. Stitch across 2 adjacent sides, using a ¼" seam allowance. Sew a narrow hem on open edge, leaving small opening at seam, forming a casing. Turn sack right side out. Place stuffing in, filling sack ⅔ of the way. Thread yarn through casing and loop around Santa's shoulders, over cape. Tie yarn ends and trim excess. Hot-glue miniatures to top of sack. Place sack on base close to body and secure to base and body with hot glue. Pull one arm around bag and secure in place with hot glue. Bend other arm and insert twig, for staff. Remove all threads and glue strings from figure. Spray lightly with acrylic spray several times, allowing figure to dry between coats.

**DIAGRAM 8**

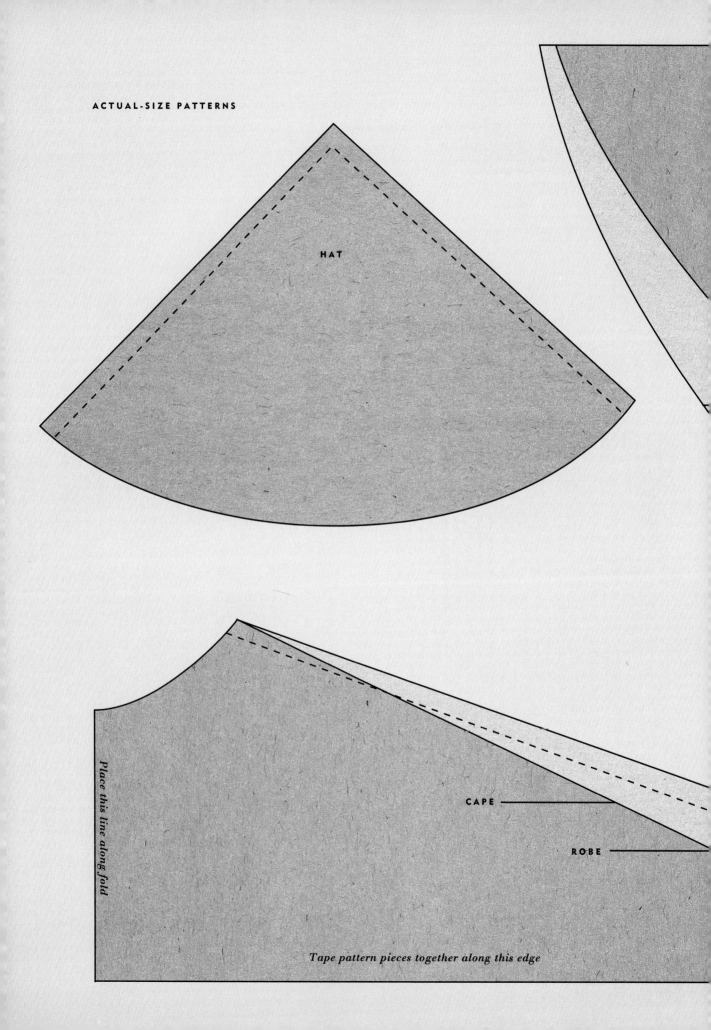

HAT

*Place this line along fold*

CAPE

ROBE

*Tape pattern pieces together along this edge*

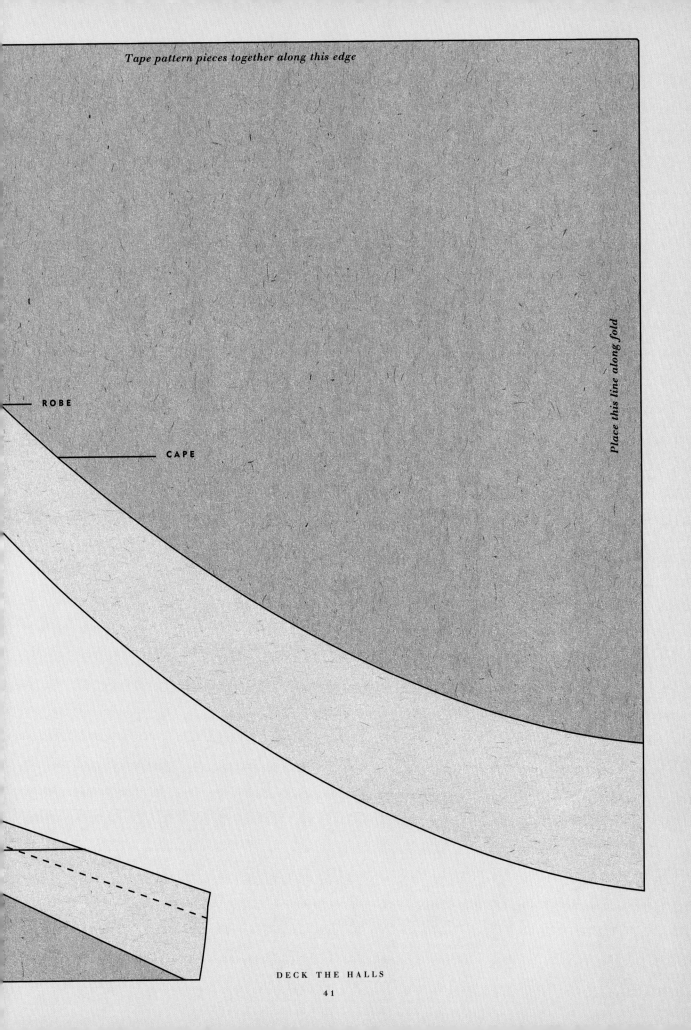

Tape pattern pieces together along this edge

ROBE

CAPE

Place this line along fold

DECK THE HALLS

41

# Natural Wonders

## OUTDOOR BEAUTY INDOORS

Let Mother Nature help you prepare the way for Father Christmas! ❖ Welcome the season by fashioning your own wreath for the front door, an inviting arrangement for your holiday table, a dressy garland for your Christmas mantel. ❖ Dry your own flowers and gather evergreens, pinecones, twigs, and moss for a delightful (and inexpensive) outdoor touch. Add a few silk flowers, artificial berries, and glossy ribbons, and paint for vibrant color and texture. To make floral arranging incredibly quick and easy, be sure to invest in a glue gun. ❖ Store your floral creations in a cool, dry place to preserve them from year to year. And if fragile flowers break off, you can replace them or add to them, making your arrangement more beautiful each year.

# HEARTY *Elf*

*Tell the world your kitchen is run by a merry elf. Hang this magical 12" wreath, fragrant with herbs and spices.*

**What You Will Need:**

Heart-shaped twig wreath, 12" in diameter

9" × 12" piece of red felt

2 scraps of ecru felt

Red sewing thread

Small amount of polyester stuffing

Bunch raffia

13–15 cinnamon sticks

9 artificial cherries

Few sprigs of juniper with berries

2 tiny black buttons or beads

Tiny red artificial berry or anther from flower
   stamen

Small bunch German statice

Small bunch dried herb (shown here, oregano; sage,
   tarragon, or rosemary may be substituted)

Pencil with eraser

Tracing paper

Scissors or shears

Sewing machine

Glue gun and glue sticks

*Note: Read How to Use a Hot Glue Gun, page 47, and How to Use Dried Florals, page 50.*

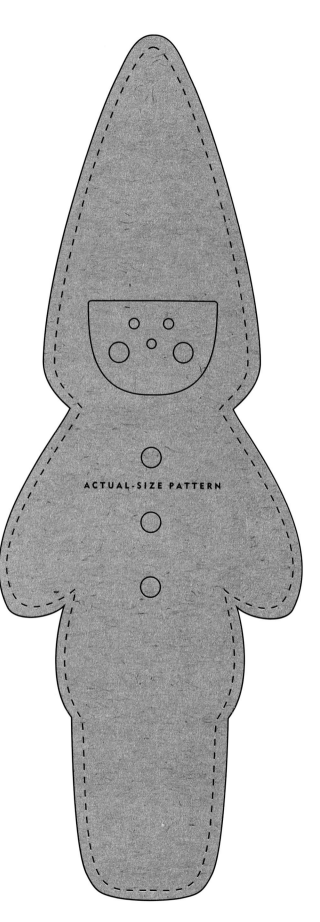

ACTUAL-SIZE PATTERN

**Prepare Wreath:** Read How to Hang a Wreath, on page 55, and attach hanger to back of wreath.

**Construct Elf:** Trace actual-size pattern for elf on tracing paper and cut out. Use pattern to cut 2 elf pieces from red felt. Also from red felt, cut two ¼" circles, for cheeks. Cut out face from pattern and use to cut one piece from ecru felt. Hot-glue face to one red elf piece (front), referring to pattern for position. Hot-glue features to face: black buttons or beads for eyes, tiny red berry or anther for nose, red felt circles for cheeks. Place front elf piece on remaining piece (back), wrong sides together. Stitch around, using ⅛" seam allowances, leaving bottom edge open. Stuff lightly, using eraser end of pencil to push stuffing into cap. Use hot glue to attach 2 small strips cut from cinnamon sticks in an X above face. Hot-glue 3 juniper berries down elf's body, for buttons, and attach 1 juniper berry to point of cap.

**Decorate Wreath:** Wrap raffia around wreath form, beginning and ending at bottom point. Hot-glue to secure. Holding 10 strands of raffia together, tie a simple bow. Hot-glue bowknot to bottom of wreath, and trim streamer ends even. Make another bow with 4 strands of raffia, and attach at center top of heart.

Following photo on page 42, hot-glue elf to center bottom of wreath. Hot-glue cinnamon sticks on bowknot and along wreath to either side of bow. Hot-glue cherries, juniper berries, statice, and dried herbs on and around bowknot and cinnamon sticks.

# *Trinket* WREATH

*Tiny Santas and even miniatures from last year's Advent calendar can add whimsical touches to this glittering 11" wreath.*

**What You Will Need:**
Grapevine wreath, 11" in diameter
2 yards red organdy ribbon, 3" wide
15–17 small red Christmas ball ornaments
7–10 miniature toys such as Santas, mushroom birds, soldiers, and candy canes
13–15 preserved or artificial holly leaves
1 handful dried German statice

Green glitter spray, or spray adhesive and green glitter
Florist's wire
Scissors
Glue gun and glue sticks

*Note: Read How to Use a Hot Glue Gun, page 47, and How to Use Dried Florals, page 50*

**Prepare Wreath and Bows:** Read How to Hang a Wreath, on page 55, and attach hanger to back of wreath. Cut ribbon into 18" lengths. Tie each in a simple bow making loops 3" long. Cut an inverted V-shape into each streamer end.

**Arrange Wreath:** Hot-glue bows along top half of wreath form. Hot-glue holly leaves around and in between bows. Use strands of wire to attach ball ornaments to top half of wreath form, on and around bows. Hot-glue miniatures to ribbons, particularly on bowknots. Use statice to fill in any spaces and to add fullness.

**Finish:** Lightly spray decorated section of wreath with green glitter, following manufacturer's instructions.

# *Apple* BIRDHOUSE

*This country-style 3" ornament is sure to become the apple of your eye!*

**What You Will Need:**

Wood apple birdhouse, 3" in diameter

2–3 silk leaves on wired stems

Mushroom bird, 1½" tall

Metallic red, olive green, and cream acrylic paints

Small flat and tapered paintbrushes

Glue gun and glue sticks

*Note: Read How to Use a Hot Glue Gun, page 47.*

**Select Substitutes:** If you can't locate a pre-cut apple birdhouse in the wood section of a craft store, you may find a wooden apple. Clamp apple to worktable, and use ¾" bit to drill doorway opening centered on side of apple. Use ¼" bit to drill hole for perch, ¼" below doorway. Insert short length of twig into this hole. A mushroom bird is an artificial bird fashioned partly, at least, from dried fungi; it can be found in the floral material section of craft stores and florist's shops. Feel free to substitute any artificial bird of your choice.

**Paint:** Remove perch from apple and set aside. Paint apple red, excluding stem. Let dry. Use olive green to paint stem and perch, and add striations to apple. Paint "bite" depression in apple with cream paint. When that is dry, paint olive green teardrop-shaped seeds in depression, as shown in photo.

**Assemble:** Dab end of perch with hot glue and reattach. Also using hot glue, attach leaves and mushroom bird to top of apple or to perch. To create a hanging ornament, thread a piece of ribbon or wire through stem hole, or insert an eyelet screw at top.

# *Hearts* AND FLOWERS

*Dainty little (2½") no-sew ornaments are a sweet accent anywhere you place them.*

**What You Will Need For Each Ornament:**

Prestuffed heart shape, 2½", with adhesive on front surface, such as Stick 'N' Puff (see Sources)

3½" square of red-and-white fabric

¼ yard red-and-green ribbon rose trim

3" square of white or green felt

¾ yard red satin ribbon, ⅛" wide

2 small sprigs of dried small white flowers such as Austrian (or alpine) daisies

2 plastic ladybugs or ladybug buttons

Scissors

Glue gun and glue sticks

*Note: Read How to Use a Hot Glue Gun, right.*

**Cover Surface:** Follow manufacturer's directions for covering heart with fabric. Cut felt to same shape and use glue gun to adhere felt to back.

**Decorate:** Cut a ribbon rose from rose trim and set aside. Beginning at top center, encircle heart with remaining rose trim, securing it to edges with glue gun. Hot-glue a sprig of white flowers to front of heart. Cover dab of glue with remaining ribbon rose.

**Finish:** Fold satin ribbon in half. Knot 2½" from fold to form a hanging loop. Secure knot at top center of heart with hot glue. Tie ribbon ends in a bow. Hot-glue ladybugs to conceal glue and/or where desired.

# HOW TO
# *Use a Hot Glue Gun*

A hot glue gun is a very handy tool. You plug it in, insert a glue stick in the back, and let it heat up for about 3 minutes. As the glue stick passes through the barrel of the gun, the heat inside melts the adhesive. When you push the glue gun trigger, liquefied glue is released from the nozzle.

The advantage of a hot glue gun is that hot glue bonds items almost immediately as it cools and it dries in seconds. There is no need to hold or tape items in place for several minutes until the glue sets, as with regular glues. You can apply a dab of glue, or keep your finger pressed on the trigger and draw out a line of glue. A glue gun is neat, but you should still protect the work surface from the minimal glue drips that occur. After glue is thoroughly cooled, remove any strings of glue. A glue gun is safe for adults to use—as long as you follow the manufacturer's instructions. Some safety tips:

❖ Most important, do not touch the hot glue or you will be burned.

❖ Keep a bowl of ice water handy so that you can immerse a burned finger immediately and prevent blistering.

❖ When you apply glue, hold item so that your fingers are as far away from glue as possible.

❖ Use a craft stick or toothpick to push items into glue, or to shift their positions.

❖ If your glue gun does not have a stand, put it down on a sheet of aluminum foil.

❖ Keep children away from hot glue guns.

If a hot glue gun makes you anxious, a low-temperature glue gun, with low-temp glue sticks, may be a better investment. You won't get the ease and super-bonding qualities, but you also won't get burned. With supervision, children can use low-temp glue guns. Also, the low-temp glue won't melt plastic foam.

## HOME *Tweet* HOME

*In less than 10 minutes, bring a cheerful cardinal home to roost in this charming, 4"-high ornament.*

**What You Will Need:**

Bark birdhouse ornament, 3" high

Artificial cardinal, 2" high

Small amount of green sphagnum moss

Few sprigs of small red berries

Hoarfrost or iridescent glitter

Spray adhesive

Glue gun and glue sticks

*Note: Read How to Use a Hot Glue Gun, page 47.*

**Assemble:** Using hot glue, attach small amounts of moss over door and to front of rooftop. Secure cardinal to moss with hot glue. Dab stems of berries with hot glue and insert them under moss above door and on roof.

**Create Snowy Effect:** Lightly spray roof and front of birdhouse with spray adhesive. Sprinkle with hoarfrost or iridescent glitter.

## *Cardinal* GARLAND

*String a medley of birds and tidbits across a mantel or doorway. Vary the number of items to adjust the length of your garland (here about 72" long).*

**What You Will Need:**

Thick wood cut-out hearts: four 2", two 2½"

Round wood beads: 8 large (¾" in diameter),
   20 medium (⅝"), 20 small (⁵⁄₁₆")

Red acrylic paint

16 cinnamon sticks

1 yard green-and-tan check craft ribbon, 2" wide

3 miniature bark birdhouses, 3" high

12 dried apple slices

3 small artificial cardinals, 2" high

4 small artificial cardinals, 2" high, in nests

6 small (3"–3½") pinecones

15–17 miniature pinecones

36–40 small artificial raspberries

10–12 small twigs

Approximately 50 small silk ivy leaves

Handful of sphagnum moss

Florist's spool wire

Ten ⅛" eyelet screws

Small flat paintbrush

Scissors

Wire cutters

String

Glue gun and glue sticks

*Note: Read How to Use a Hot-Glue Gun,
page 47.*

**Prepare Decorations:** String beads and set up a makeshift clothesline, so that you can paint all surfaces at once. Paint hearts and beads red. Let dry. Paint reverse sides of hearts.

Divide cinnamon sticks into 4 bundles of 4. Cut ribbon into 4 equal pieces. Wrap each bundle with a piece of ribbon. Tie knot and cut streamer ends on an angle.

Hot-glue a small amount of moss to roof of each birdhouse. Hot-glue a bird to moss. Add twigs, ivy leaves, miniature pinecones, and/or raspberries as embellishments.

Hot-glue 3 apple slices together in a stack. Hot-glue a nested bird to top of slices, adding bits of moss, ivy, and berries.

Attach eyelet screws at top center on 2 small hearts, to both upper sides of 2 small hearts, at lower left and upper right of 1 large heart, and at lower right and upper left of remaining large heart.

**Form Garland:** Use one birdhouse as center. Force florist's wire through birdhouse below roof, until 6" of wire extends from either side of birdhouse. Using wire cutters, cut wire from spool. Onto each wire extension slide a small, medium, and large wood bead. Insert wire ends through eyelet ring at upper side of a small heart, bending wire end back and twisting it around itself several times. Cut off excess wire.

Using wire cutters, cut two 18" lengths of wire. Attach one to eyelet screw on opposite side of each small heart. Force wire through bird's nest

on stacked apple slices, then add 1 small bead, a medium bead, a cinnamon bundle, a medium bead, 2 small beads, another birdhouse, 3 small beads, a medium bead, a pinecone (wrapping wire around a row of scales), a medium bead, and a small bead. Attach end of wire to upper eyelet ring at side of a large heart. Trim excess wire.

Using wirecutters, cut two 22" lengths of wire. Attach one to lower eyelet ring on opposite side of each large heart. Thread each wire through large bead, medium bead, pinecone, a medium bead, a large bead, a cinnamon bundle, a large bead, a medium bead, a small bead, a bird's nest on apple slices, a medium bead, a pinecone, a medium bead, a small bead, and upper eyelet ring on side of a small heart. Trim excess wire.

**Finish:** Using hot glue, decorate the pinecones with ivy leaves, moss, and raspberries. Use ivy leaves, moss, and miniature pinecones to decorate the hearts. Use hot glue to secure moss over eyelet screws to conceal them.

## HOW TO
# *Use Dried Florals*

❖ Dried florals—flowers, berries, ferns, leaves, grasses, etc.—are often brittle and break easily. Make sure you have more than you need for a project, as some will fall apart in handling.

❖ Use kitchen scissors to clip stems to the lengths you desire. If you're inserting the flowers into foam, use soft gray florist's foam. Cut stems an inch longer than you want them, and hold each stem close to the end as you insert it into the foam. If stems are fragile, first attach to florist's wire using florist's tape.

❖ You may wish to spray finished pieces with clear acrylic sealer, to strengthen and protect fragile florals and make them last for more than a season.

❖ When creating any floral arrangement, from a small spray on a wreath to a large bouquet in a basket, first establish an overall shape and a focal point—usually at the center or just off center of the overall shape. Let secondary and filler florals echo the shape, or radiate outward from the focal point to call attention to it. Trust your eye as to scale and color.

❖ Work with 1 type of floral material at a time. Distribute it all over the piece before proceeding to the next. Using odd numbers of items—3 roses rather than 2, for example—usually results in the best balance. It is helpful to start with the biggest, tallest, or most prominent elements of the composition, then proceed to the smallest. Use small or feathery items as filler, in spaces between larger florals, or to lighten the general feeling of the arrangement.

# *Winter* BASKET

*Perfect for a rectangular or oval dining table, this distinctive 11" centerpiece is low enough to encourage conversations across the table.*

**What You Will Need:**

Dark green basket, approximately 11" long and 5" high, with or without handle

Assorted dried florals, including:

    6–10 white freeze-dried roses

    6–10 small bunches Austrian daisies

    8–10 stems canella berries

    8–10 dried red peppers

    Few stems silver artemesia

    Few stems dried maidenhair fern

    Small bunch preserved cedar

    Spanish moss

    8–10 small assorted twigs

    3–4 pinecones

    2–3 dried cotton hulls

Brick of gray florist's foam

Kitchen knife

Glue gun and glue sticks

*Note: Read How to Use a Hot Glue Gun, page 47, and How to Use Dried Florals, left.*

**Prepare Basket:** If your basket is unpainted, you may wish to spray-paint it.

**Arrange Florals:** If necessary, trim foam with a kitchen knife so that it is no more than 1" higher than basket rim. Hot-glue foam to bottom of basket, off-center. Tuck Spanish moss around sides and

"*O Christmas tree,*

*O Christmas tree,*

*How lovely are thy branches.*"

edges of foam, and spread it loosely on top to conceal foam. Insert stem ends of cedar in sides of foam so that cedar spills over rim on all sides. Place a few pieces of cedar in an upright position on one side of basket, establishing a large triangular shape for arrangement. Place maidenhair fern evenly among cedar pieces, securing with hot glue.

For a focal point, arrange pinecones and cotton hulls in a triangle at center of foam, and secure in place with hot glue. Hot-glue roses in and around this focal point. Referring to photo, add remaining botanicals. Distribute red and white colors around and radiating outward from the focal point. With each floral material, subtly echo the triangular formations.

# *Candle* RING

*Revive the Swedish tradition of the Santa Lucia wreath with this lively 12" arrangement of florals and candles.*

**What You Will Need:**

Wire hearts candle ring*, 12" in diameter

1 yard red-and-green tartan ribbon, 1½" wide

    15–18 artificial red cherries

    18–20 artificial frosted cherries with leaves

    8–10 assorted small berries

    4–5 artificial raspberries

    20–25 small pinecones

    Bunch dried baby's breath

    Small bunch preserved cedar or pine

4 red 10"–12" candle tapers

Scissors or shears

Glue gun and glue sticks

\* If you cannot locate this or similar wire ring, substitute a wire or twig wreath form and hot-glue 4 candle cups (to hold tapers) securely into form.

*Note: Read How to Use a Hot Glue Gun, page 47, and How to Use Dried Florals, page 50.*

**Form Bow:** Cut a 15" and 30" length from ribbon. At center of each, tie a simple bow with 2½"-long loops. Cut each streamer end in an inverted V-shape. Hot-glue knot of bow with short streamers to knot of bow with long streamers. Glue that knot to bottom of 1 wire heart. Loosely wrap long streamers around wire wreath base, securing in place with dots of hot glue.

**Arrange Florals:** Hot-glue dried and artificial florals and fruits around base of candle ring, in a solid wreath. Position materials so that they radiate outward all around. Begin with greenery. Use cherries, berries, and cones, to conceal hot glue. Finish by adding tapers.

# *Pretty* POUCHES

*Embellish these attractive 4" ornaments with a variety of natural touches, from pinecones to dried pods, rosebuds, nutmeg, nuts in the shell, feathers, and seashells.*

**What You Will Need For Each Pouch:**

Plastic foam ball, 3" in diameter

Small amount of red-and-green cotton fabric or felt

½ yard of wide (1" or 1½") satin ribbon

⅜ yard of narrow (⅜") ribbon or satin cording

One or more of the following trims: several miniature pinecones, small artificial berry cluster with leaves, gold-plated pin or charm

Scissors and pinking shears

Glue gun and glue sticks

*Note: Read How to Use a Hot Glue Gun, page 47.*

**Make Hanging Loop:** Cut an 8" length of narrow ribbon. Fold crosswise in half, and use scissors' tip to poke ribbon ends into plastic foam ball. Dab on hot glue to secure loop at base.

**Cover Ball:** From fabric, use pinking shears to cut a circle 12" in diameter. (It may be helpful to trace around a 10" dinner plate and cut 1" beyond marked line all around.) Place plastic foam ball in center of fabric circle. Draw fabric up around ball so that hanging loop emerges at top. Secure fabric with narrow and/or wide ribbon tied in a bow.

**Embellish Ball:** Hot-glue floral or artificial trims to knot of bow. If desired, use hot glue to secure remaining narrow ribbon under bow, for additional streamers. Cut streamer ends in an inverted V-shape or at an angle.

# *Potpourri* WREATH

*In years to come, revive the scent of this fragrant 13"
wreath with a spritz of pine room freshener or a dab
of vanilla.*

**What You Will Need:**

Plastic foam wreath base, 12" in diameter

16 ounces Christmas potpourri with pinecones

1 yard red-and-gold paper ribbon, 2¾" wide

1 yard red paper ribbon, 1½" wide

Wire clothes hanger and florist's wire, for hanger

Scissors

Tacky glue

Glue gun and glue sticks

*Note: Read How to Use a Hot Glue Gun, page 47.*

**Prepare Wreath:** Read How to Hang a Wreath
on page 55, and attach a hanger.

**Cover Wreath:** Set aside a handful of potpourri.
Pick out most of the pinecones from remaining
potpourri and set aside. Working in sections, cover
front and side surfaces of wreath with tacky glue
and gently press the remaining potpourri on top.
Let dry. Apply hot glue to base of pinecones and
apply them individually, spacing evenly all around,
but omitting at center bottom.

**Form Bows:** Using wide paper ribbon, make a
simple bow with 3½" loops and 4" streamers.
Cut streamer ends in an inverted V-shape. Using
hot glue, secure bow to bottom of wreath. Carefully
hot-glue potpourri, one item at a time, over bow
knot, and continue filling in any empty spaces
around or under bow using this method.

Cut remaining ribbon into four 6" pieces. Creasing
only 1 side, accordion-fold each piece of ribbon to
create 3 loops, one on top of the other. Hot-glue
creased side of looped ribbon under bow streamers
on each side so loops radiate outward.

# Poinsettia WREATH

*For welcoming color and a classy touch, combine vivid silk flowers with subtler dried materials. Everyone will notice this 16" wreath!*

**What You Will Need:**

Green plastic foam wreath form, 12" in diameter

7–8 silk poinsettia heads

Bunch dried or preserved greens (such as fern or boxwood) for filler

1 bunch dried baby's breath

Stub wire and craft ribbon scrap, for hanging loop

Glue gun and glue sticks

*Note: Read How to Use a Hot Glue Gun, page 47 and How to Use Dried Florals, page 50.*

**Prepare Wreath:** Read How to Hang a Wreath, right, and attach hanger to wreath form.

**Arrange Flowers:** Cut poinsettia stems to 1" at base of flower heads. Insert stems into foam wreath, using hot glue to secure and spacing flowers evenly. Break off small sprigs of green florals and baby's breath. Dab stems with hot glue, and insert them around and under the poinsettias so that they radiate outward. Also make use of these filler-type florals to conceal foam wreath base.

# HOW TO
# Hang a Wreath

Always attach the hanger to your wreath before you start working on the front of it. This way, you won't ever have to rest the wreath on its front and risk damaging fragile floral materials.

**Attaching a Hanger to Wreath Back**

Start with a 6" length of stiff wire—24-gauge stub wire for a lightweight wreath, or, for a heavier wreath, the hook of a clothes hanger, bent back and forth until it snaps off. With pliers, bend wire into a wide horseshoe shape.

To attach to a foam or lightweight wreath, position hanger on wreath and apply a generous blob of hot glue across wire ends. Immediately cover hot glue with craft ribbon to conceal the blob.

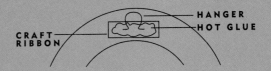

To attach to a twig wreath or base that will support more weight, use florist's wire or thin spool wire. Wrap each horseshoe end, then wrap around the wreath form. If twig wreath base will show in front, wrap wire around one or two twigs only.

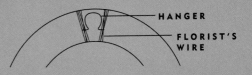

**Attaching a Hanging Loop at Wreath Top**

Wrap florists' wire around wreath form. Twist at top (but not so tightly that wire cuts through foam or base), and then wrap around again to secure wire. Twist ends together to form loop at top. This method works best with heavier wreaths where florals or other decorations will hide the wire.

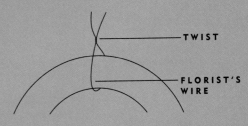

# *Della Robbia* GARLAND

*A lavish arch of pinecones, fruit, and birds in warm and frosted shades spans 28" and dresses up a frame with graceful elegance.*

**What You Will Need:**

3 large (15") sprays of assorted artificial fruit and
  berries

4 yards brown/green velvet ribbon, 1" wide

32–35 small pinecones

10–12 white-tipped pinecones

3 mushroom or artificial birds

Small bird's nest

2 bunches preserved ferns

Florist's tape

Florist's wire

Scissors

Glue gun and glue sticks

*Note: Read How to Use a Hot Glue Gun, page 47, and How to Use Dried Florals, page 50.*

**Build Foundation:** Begin garland at center and work outward on both sides. Hold 2 floral sprays horizontally, with stem ends together and overlapping for 2", and fruit facing outward on either side. Wrap overlapped section of stems tightly with florist's tape to secure. Gently bend sprays downward to form an arch.

**Add Ribbons:** Cut a 1-yard length and a 15" length from ribbon and set aside. Use remaining ribbon to form a 6-loop bow following directions in How to Make a Multi-Loop Bow, on page 90. Start 27" from one end and make loops 3" long. Notch an inverted V into each streamer end. Tie 15" length of ribbon around bow center and cut streamer ends in same manner. Spread 1-yard length of ribbon across garland, centering. Place 6-loop bow on top, and use wire ends and hot glue to secure bow to center of garland, catching 1-yard length of ribbon in the process. Drape and loop longest streamers among the fruit and greenery, securing in place with hot glue. Keep shorter streamers free for hanging.

**Arrange Florals:** Remove fruit and berries from third spray by gently pulling wires out of main stem. Using hot glue and wrapping wired stems, attach greenery, pinecones, and additional fruit and berries from third spray to garland. Position heaviest concentration of items at center of garland. Bend stems so that fruit extends outward. Hot-glue one bird in bird's nest and attach nest near bow. Attach remaining birds to garland, well spaced; see photo for suggested positions.

**Hang:** To attach garland to mirror or picture frame, affix a long strand of florist's wire to garland at back, starting appproximately 2" from one end of arch. Run wire along back of garland, following arch. Twist wire around garland to affix about every 4", so that there are a total of 6 points of contact between wire and garland. Pull wires back, away from garland, and hook over top corners of frame to hold garland in place.

> *"Oh Tidings of Comfort and Joy,*
>
> *Comfort and Joy,*
>
> *Oh Tidings of Comfort and Joy"*

# Crafted With Love
## GIFTS FROM THE HEART

*Giving just the right gift to someone special is one of the greatest joys in life.* ❖ *And a well-chosen present becomes even more special when it has been handmade by you. In this section you will find a wide variety of suggestions for gifts: something for everyone on your list.* ❖ *Create decorative picture frames, stitch together an adorable Christmasaurus, craft elegant jewelry, or hand-paint a charming tea set.* ❖ *Whatever project you choose to make, do not hesitate to adapt the colors or materials to personalize your gift. And find some spot—whether hidden or not—on which to sign your name and the date.*

# *Memento* FRAMES

*Inexpensive little collectibles give any framed picture vintage charm and a personal touch.*

**What You Will Need:**

Super-strength epoxy glue

Photograph

*For Key Frame:*

    11" × 14" wood frame

    5" × 7" mat to fit photo and frame

    Several old keys (11 used on frame shown)

*For Button Frame*

    Thin metal rectangular picture frame

    Oval picture mat to fit frame

    Large assortment of old buttons

    Pliers

**Embellish Frames:** Use pliers to remove shanks from buttons without sew-through holes. Arrange keys or buttons to corners of photo frame or over glass that covers mat. Overlap items, and play with various arrangements until you are satisfied. Using epoxy, secure keys or buttons to surfaces.

**Insert Picture:** Following manufacturer's instructions, place photo behind mat and insert both into frame.

> *"I'll be home for Christmas,*
>
> *You can count on me.*
>
> *Please have snow, and mistletoe,*
>
> *And presents on the tree."*

# *Fish* FRAME

*Give someone who loves fishing this personalized frame, approximately 7" × 9", to show off a very special catch.*

**What You Will Need:**

Wood frame with edges at least 1½" wide and
    4" × 6" window

5" × 7" sheet of copper

Eight ¼" brass brads

Glue

Small hammer

*Items listed in How to Cut and Pierce Metal, page 11*

**Prepare Fish:** Read How to Cut and Pierce Metal, on page 11. Following directions and using actual-size pattern at right, cut 4 fish shapes from copper. Pound flat with mallet. Use awl to make holes: one at eye position, another at center of tail fin.

**Assemble:** Remove glass from frame. Position fish as desired on frame. Glue in place, then hammer brads into holes. Place glass back in frame once fish is in place.

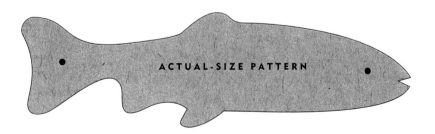

**ACTUAL-SIZE PATTERN**

# *Patchwork* FRAME

*Any snapshot or postcard is picture-perfect in this no-sew, 11" × 14" mosaic of fabric prints.*

**What You Will Need:**

Self-stick mounting board, 11" × 14", available from Pres-On Merchandising Corp. (see Sources)

Picture mat 5" × 7" (outside dimensions), in desired color

Snapshot, greeting card, postcard, or mirror 3½" × 5"

Scraps of assorted print fabrics

Passementerie trim, ⅛" wide: 2¼ yards red-and-gold, 1½ yards gold

Florist's wire

White craft glue

Glue gun and glue sticks

Pencil

Ruler

*Note: Read How to Use a Hot Glue Gun, page 47.*

**Prepare Mat and Fabrics:** Center mat on back of mounting board. Using pencil, trace around mat. Set mat aside. Use ruler to divide area outside of mat into rectangles as shown in diagram. Cut fabrics into 12 rectangular patches each 3½" × 4". Arrange them to your satisfaction in marked areas around mounting board. Trim 4 patches, for center of shorter sides, to 3" × 4". Press edges of patches ¼" to wrong side.

**Assemble:** Measure and mark rectangles to correspond with diagram on sticky side of mounting board. Position patches on sticky side of board. If necessary, secure edges and corners of patches with a small amount of craft glue. Center snapshot, card, or mirror on mounting board. Hot-

glue mat, centered, on top. Hot-glue red and gold trim around mat and around mounting board, on front surfaces. Hot-glue gold trim on edges all around.

**Prepare for Hanging:** Make a horseshoe shape with a 6" length of florist's wire. Hot-glue ends of wire to back of frame.

**DIAGRAM FOR PATCHWORK FRAME**

# *Treasure* KEEPER

*Covered with style, this 4" wooden box makes a fine nest for small pieces of jewelry. The padded lid provides a place to stick pins.*

**What You Will Need:**

Heart-shaped wood box with lid, 4"–5" wide

Small amounts of felt

Small amounts of 2 coordinating fabric prints

Soft 2" or 3" heart with self-adhesive backing such as Stik 'N' Puff (see Sources)

2 yards red-and-green thin (1/16") twisted cord

1/2 yard pleated ribbon, 1/2" wide, or jumbo rickrack

Tacky glue with applicator tip

Fine felt-tip marker

Scissors

Flat paintbrush

**Cover Box:** Using marker, trace box bottom onto felt. Cut out and set aside. Cut a 2" × 15" strip from one fabric (Fabric 1). Pour about 3 tablespoons of glue into a margarine container or jar lid. Use a paintbrush to apply a thin coating of glue onto sides of box. Starting at center top of heart and placing one long edge even with rim of box, wrap strip around box. Trim opposite short end so that ends butt. Paint glue on edges at box bottom. Bring excess fabric to box bottom, clipping around curves and at angles to avoid bulk, and press into glue. Brush glue on felt heart and adhere it to box bottom.

**Cover Lid:** Trace box lid onto coordinating fabric (Fabric 2); cut out, adding 1/2" all around. Brush top of lid with glue and center fabric heart on top. Brush sides of lid with glue. Clip into excess fabric at curves and angles, and press down onto glue.

From felt, cut a strip to width and circumference of sides of lid. Brush with glue and adhere, starting and ending at top center of heart. Follow manufacturer's directions for covering soft sticky-back heart; use Fabric 1. Center covered heart on lid; hot-glue in place.

**Add Trim:** Squeeze glue from its applicator tip to apply trim. Start and end at center top of heart shape. First, glue pleated ribbon or rickrack around center of sides of lid. Glue twisted cord centered on top of this trim and around edge of soft heart. Use remaining twisted cord to tie a simple bow, and glue to center top of soft heart.

*"I have no gift to bring*

*pa rum pum pum pum*

*That's fit to give a king*

*pa rum pum pum pum"*

# *Thimble* SET

*All you need is a steady hand to customize these tiny wood thimbles (1") and needle case (2¼").*

**What You Will Need:**

Wood thimbles

Wood needle case, 2¼" high

Red and green acrylic paints

Pencil

Gold fine felt-tip marker

Fine, tapered paintbrush

**Add Motifs:** As motifs are too small to transfer, refer to actual-size patterns as a guide only, and practice on scrap paper first, drawing and painting motifs freehand. Pencil in approximate outlines. Dip only tip of paintbrush into paint, and apply carefully over and between pencil outlines. Measure circumference of thimble or needle case, and plan how many motifs, evenly spaced, you can fit around sides. You should be able to fit 3 bows around needle case and 3 bows or 5 holly motifs around thimble. Pencil according to plan.

Also pencil a motif on top of thimble or needle case cap. Paint motifs using one color at a time. Let paint dry before painting alongside it in another color.

**Finish:** Paint rims of thimbles and rim band of needle case. Complete design with dots: Paint or mark dots in gold, red, or green around sides of needle case and between motifs, as space permits.

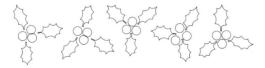

# *Sewing* BOX

*This box, 9" wide, 7" deep, and 5¼" high, is modeled after old Norwegian trinket holders, but your handiwork gives it its own special look.*

**What You Will Need:**

1 oval wood box with lid and handles, medium "Oval Tine" from Designs by Bentwood, Inc. (see Sources)

¼ yard fabric (here, red check print)

9" × 12" piece felt

Red and green acrylic paints

Flat paintbrush

Fine felt-tip marker

Tacky glue

Scissors

**Paint Lid and Braces:** Paint box lid handle red. Let dry, then paint lid and box side braces green. Allow paint to dry thoroughly.

**Decorate Box:** Trace bottom of box on felt. Cut out and set aside. Cut two 8" × 12" rectangles from fabric. Pour about 6 tablespoons of tacky glue into a margarine container or jar lid. Use a paintbrush to apply a thin coat of glue to sides of box. Center and smooth fabric pieces in place on each side. Clip into excess fabric at 1" intervals and apply tacky glue to adhere excess fabric to inside rim and box bottom. Apply tacky glue with brush to bottom of box and smooth felt piece in place. Use scissors to trim excess felt around bottom.

*"Bearing gifts, we traverse afar,*

*Field and fountain,*

*moor and mountain*

*Following yonder star."*

# *Patchwork* PINCUSHION

*Even novice quilters will enjoy patching a mini-quilt, 7" square, to cover the top of this little basket filled with stuffing.*

**What You Will Need:**

Closely woven basket, 5" in diameter, 2" high

Foot of nylon stocking

Small amounts of assorted print fabrics

8" square of muslin

8" square of traditional quilt batting

Sewing and quilting thread

Polyester stuffing

Pencil

Ruler

Scrap of cardboard

Scissors

Straight pins

Sewing and quilting needles

Sewing machine (optional)

Iron

**Create Patchwork:** Cut a 1½" square from cardboard, for template. Use template to cut 25 patches from assorted fabrics. Arrange squares in 5 rows of 5. To join squares, pin one to another with right sides together. Stitch along one side, ¼" from raw edge. Press seam allowances to one side. Join squares together in rows. Join rows together, matching seams. You should have a piece of patchwork 5½" square. Cut two 1½" × 5½" strips from one of the fabrics and stitch one each to opposite sides of patchwork, using ¼" seam allowances. Cut two 1½" × 7½" strips of fabric and stitch one to each remaining side. Cut muslin and batting to fit bordered patchwork. Place muslin on batting, with patchwork, wrong side up, on top. Pin layers together and stitch around, ¼" from edges, leaving an opening for turning. Clip corners and turn right side out. Turn open edges to inside and slip-stitch closed. Press quilt. Quilt with little running stitches as shown in diagram.

**Stuff Cushion:** Stuff stocking so that, when placed in basket, the mound it makes will be snug to sides of basket and ½" higher than basket rim. Remove stuffed stocking. Stitch the stocking closed. Place stuffed stocking centered on wrong side of quilt. Bring up corners of quilt around it and use needle and thread to secure it around stuffed stocking. Reinsert stuffed stocking, now with a quilted cover, into basket.

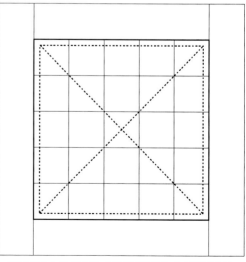

**DIAGRAM FOR QUILTING PATTERN**

# FOR HER *Lapel*

*Set off a gold-plated charm or pin with ribbons, to create a piece of jewelry (4"–5" long) that shows the world she deserves a medal.*

**What You Will Need:**
Charm or decorative pin, 1½" long
Sewing thread to match ribbons
Pin back, 1½" long
Scissors
Epoxy glue

*For Military-Style Pin:*
⅛ yard striped grosgrain ribbon, 1½" wide
Small tassel, purchased individually or from tassel trim

*For Prize-Ribbon Style Pin:*
½ yard striped grosgrain ribbon, 1" wide
Scrap of green satin wire-edge ribbon, 1½" wide
⅛ yard string of gold seed beads

**Design Military-Style Pin:** Fold ribbon crosswise in half and secure with hot glue. Pinch ends and wrap tightly with thread to gather. Tie or glue tassel over gathered ends, and glue charm or attach decorative pin on top, concealing gathered raw ends. Using epoxy, attach pin back to back of ribbon loop, ⅛" from fold.

**Design Prize-Ribbon Style Pin:** Cut a 7¼" length of striped ribbon. Fold 1 end over itself for 2¼", gluing the end to secure; cut other end in an inverted V. From remaining ribbon cut two 4" lengths. Fold each crosswise in half to form a loop, and glue ends to secure. Referring to photo, arrange ribbon: Place long piece with loop up, notched end down. Place a loop at each diagonal, with folds at top and ends overlapping center of first notched ribbon. Glue at overlap. On side of wire-edge ribbon, pull wire from both ends and gather ribbon along wire. Twist wire ends together and fan out opposite long edge. Fold ribbon ends under and glue onto grosgrain ribbon, covering raw edges. Fold string of beads in half and twist; wrap or tie ends together to form a ring, gluing to secure. Tack or glue ring at this joint to bottom of fanned-out wire-edge ribbon. Glue charm on top so that loop of beads hangs below it as shown. Glue pin back behind center top ribbon loop.

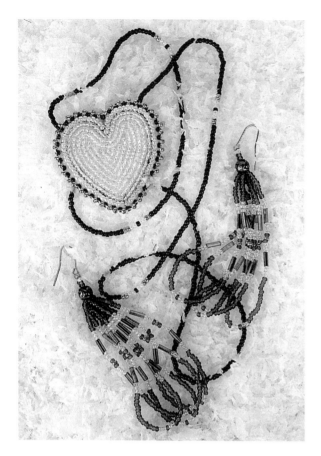

**Fill In:** Thread 30" of beading thread on needle, pull ends even and knot. Work on one felt heart shape only, using white seed beads, and working a "beading backstitch" as follows: Stitch through felt heart at center bottom, ⅛" from edge (Diagram 1). Place 4 beads on thread and slide to end. Lay threaded beads parallel to heart's edge and stitch through felt after fourth bead. Bring needle up through felt between second and third bead. Thread needle through holes of third and fourth beads to secure. See Diagram 2. Place 4 more beads on thread and lay along edge of heart in a line continuous with preceding beads. Stitch through felt, bring needle up through felt between second and third beads of this set. Thread third and fourth beads as before. Continue beading in this manner until you have an outline of beads all around felt shape.

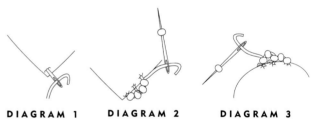

**DIAGRAM 1**    **DIAGRAM 2**    **DIAGRAM 3**

# *Seed Bead* PENDANT

............................................................

*If a lady on your list is a romantic, create a real jewel—a luminous 2¼" valentine she can wear close to her heart.*

**What You Will Need:**

7" square of white felt

Size 11 beads, 1 package each: white translucent, metallic gold, red

Size 13 beading needle

Size 0 beading thread

Straight pins

Pencil

Tracing paper

Fabric glue

Scissors

**Cut Heart:** Trace actual-size heart pattern from page 15 onto tracing paper and cut out. Pin pattern to felt; cut out 2 heart shapes.

Use concentric rounds of beading backstitch to fill in outline, working in closely aligned rounds toward center. Refer to photo: note innermost "rounds" are actually non-continuous V-shapes. Tie a double knot to finish. Trim away ⅛" felt all around beaded heart; be careful to leave all threads intact. Use fabric glue to attach beaded heart to second heart shape, for backing. Allow glue to set and cut backing to same size as front.

**Add Edge:** Make edge-lace stitches as follows, referring to Diagram 3: Thread 40" of thread onto needle, pull ends even, and knot. Take a tiny stitch at edge of felt shape, stitching through both layers of felt. Thread 1 red, 1 gold, and 1 red bead onto needle, and slide to end of thread. Take a stitch into felt, then bring needle up through last red bead again. String on 1 gold and 1 red bead, then stitch into felt, coming up through last red bead. Continue in this manner, attaching only red beads to the felt, until heart is completely outlined with this beaded edging.

Manipulate spacing so that pattern is not disrupted when you come fully around to the beginning—end with a gold bead. Finish by threading needle through first red bead, both felt pieces, back through red bead, then next 2 beads and felt; fasten off with a knot and clip thread end close to surface.

**Bead Cord:** Thread 40" of beading thread on needle, pull ends even, and knot. Take a stitch through felt heart and through 1 red edge-lace bead at upper right lobe of beaded heart. String on red beads for 3". String on 2 gold, 2 white, 1 red, 2 white, and 2 gold beads. Add red beads to obtain a 3" section and repeat same pattern as before. Complete neck strand with a 10" red section, pattern repeat, 3" of red, pattern repeat, and 3" red section. Finish necklace by threading through a red edge-lace bead on upper left lobe of beaded heart and through felt before tying a double knot.

# *Seed Bead* EARRINGS

*To shorten these dazzling 4"-long shoulder dusters, simply use fewer beads for the long loops.*

### What You Will Need:

Size 12 beads, 1 package each: green, white translucent, gold

1 package teal green bugle beads

2 gold 9mm or 10mm beads, rose or Old World pattern

Size 13 beading needle

Size 0 beading thread

2 gold ear wires

Small flat-nosed jewelry pliers

Scissors

**Start Each Earring:** For top section: Thread 36" of thread on needle. Use as a single strand and do not knot end. Pull only 5–6" of thread through needle eye. Insert large gold bead onto needle and slide to 5" from opposite end of thread. Add 2 green, 4 white translucent, and 2 green seed beads. Thread needle back through top of gold bead as shown in diagram, pulling thread through to form a loop of beads. Tie the 2 threads ends in 4 overlapping square knots to secure bead in place.

**Fashion Long Loops:** Add beads in the following pattern to make a 3½" section: 9 green beads, 3 white translucent, 1 bugle, 3 white translucent, 1 green, 1 gold, 1 green, 3 white translucent, 1 bugle, 3 white translucent, 15 green, 2 white translucent, 1 green (this bead will be at center and bottom of beaded loop). Work pattern in reverse: 2 white translucent, 15 green, 3 white translucent, 1 bugle, 3 white translucent, 1 green, 1 gold, 1 green, 3 white translucent, 1 bugle, 3 white translucent, 9 green. Thread needle up through gold bead and through each bead of top loop. Thread needle back through gold bead. Tie a single knot using both threads. In this manner, make 3 additional long loops. Tie a double knot to finish, and insert needle back through 1½" of beads on any loop. Clip excess thread. Thread needle onto remaining loose thread end and through 1½" of beads on one loop. Clip excess thread.

**Assemble:** Using pliers, open ear wire loop. Place bead loop into ear wire loop and close wire loop with pliers.

**DIAGRAM FOR EARRINGS**

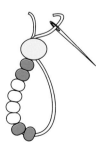

# FOR *Specs and Keys*

*No one will misplace eyeglasses or keys with this attractive needlepoint case (3½" × 6¼"), and ring fob (1¼" × 3"). Substitute any trio of colors you wish.*

**What You Will Need:**

White needlepoint canvas, 10 mesh-to-the-inch: 9" square for each

DMC tapestry yarn, Article 486: 2 skeins each red #7138 and green #7383, and 1 skein ecru for eyeglass case; 1 skein each color for key ring

Metal key ring, 1¼" in diameter

*Equipment listed in How to Needlepoint, page 17.*

**SStart Needlepoint:** Read How to Needlepoint on page 17. Cut canvas square in half for key ring. Following general instructions, tape edges of canvas pieces. Begin working at lower right corner, 1" from bottom and right edges. Use continental stitch, working all areas in green first, then red, then ecru. Follow individual directions below.

**Stitch Eyeglass Case:** For each horizontal row, follow chart from A to B, then work from C to A, to work back of case simultaneously. Work rows from D to E, then work rows from E to F 10

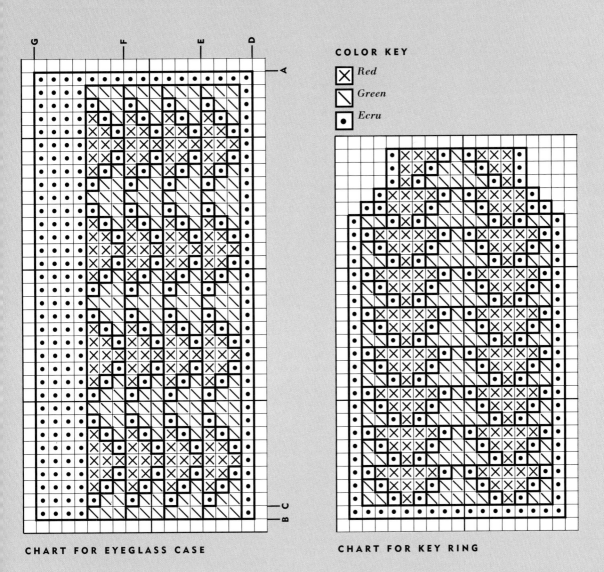

**CHART FOR EYEGLASS CASE**

**CHART FOR KEY RING**

**COLOR KEY**

☒ Red

◪ Green

· Ecru

times, then work from F to G. You will have a total of 22 horizontal rows of triangles.

Fold over ecru stripe at top and tack to back with a few stitches, taking care that they not show through to right side. Fold needlepoint lengthwise in half with wrong side in, and join side and bottom edge with overcast stitches.

**Stitch Key Fob:** Following chart, work each piece of canvas identically. Slip key ring onto narrow end of fob before finishing those edges with overcast stitches.

**Finish:** When needlepointing is completed, trim canvas to within 3 rows of needlework. Fold under unstitched areas of canvas, leaving just 1 empty mesh all around. Place front on back, wrong sides together. To join edges, use ecru yarn and overcast-stitch along empty row of mesh. Strive to follow diagonal direction of continental stitches.

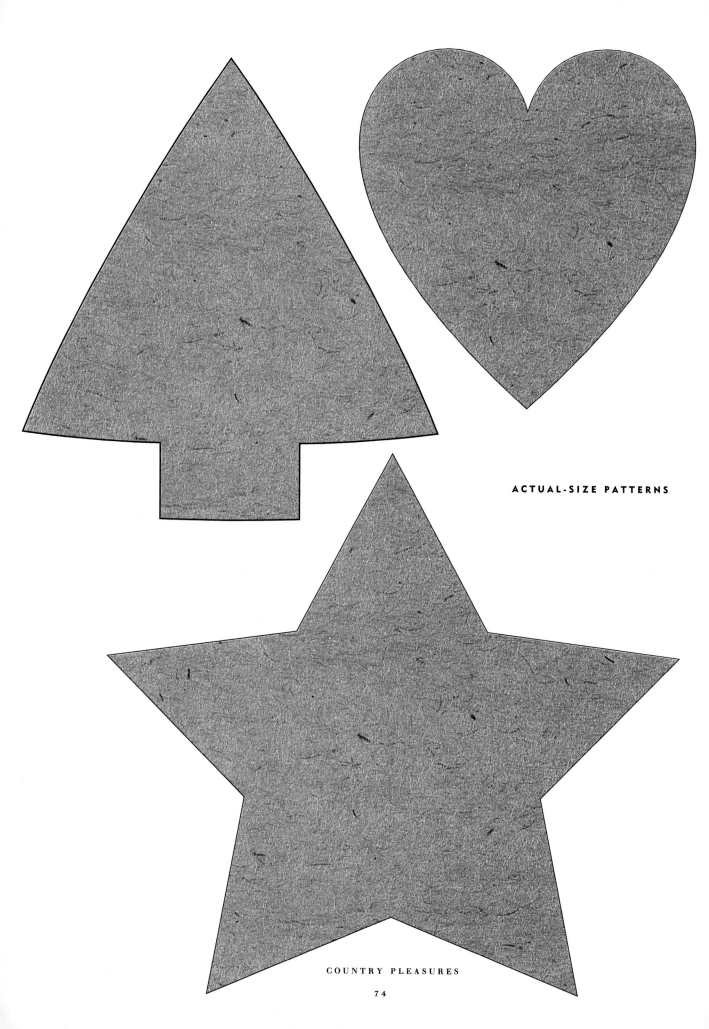

# Holiday SACHETS

*Scent a corner of a room or a lingerie drawer with these simply charming 3¼"–5" shapes. Add hanging loops and present as ornaments or pomanders.*

**What You Will Need:**

Scraps of print fabrics

Sewing thread to match fabrics

Polyester stuffing

Christmas or other potpourri, 1 tablespoonful per sachet

Pencil with eraser

Tracing paper

Sewing needle

Sewing machine (optional)

Scissors

**Sew Sachet:** Trace actual-size patterns onto tracing paper. Cut out shapes. Fold fabric scraps in half with right sides together. Pin patterns to folded fabrics and cut out. With right sides still together, sew around, using ¼" seam allowances and leaving an opening for turning and stuffing. Clip inside curves and across corners. Turn right side out.

**Fill:** Stuff two-thirds full; make a well in stuffing and add potpourri. Continue adding stuffing until plump; use eraser end of pencil to push stuffing into corners. Turn open edges to inside and slip-stitch closed.

# *Christmasaurus*

*A dino-loving tyke will adore this 20"-long stuffed brontosaurus in Christmas red and green.*

**What You Will Need:**
½ yard red-and-white checked poly/cotton fabric
Sewing thread to match fabric
1 yard green satin ribbon, ⅞" wide
Pair of teddy bear buttons for eyes
Polyester stuffing
Sewing needle
Straight pins
Sewing machine
Sharp scissors

**Cut Patterns:** Enlarge patterns 400% by photocopying at 200% twice. Use actual-size patterns to cut pieces from fabric: 2 body pieces, 4 front leg pieces, and 4 back leg pieces; patterns include ⅜" seam allowances.

**Sew Pieces:** Pin pieces together in matching pairs with right sides together. As instructed below, sew all around, using ⅜" seam allowances and leaving open between small circles as drawn on patterns. Clip into seam allowances along curves at clip marks as shown. Turn pieces right side out.

In this manner, join pieces for 2 pairs of legs; see Diagram 1. Pin unstuffed legs to right sides of body pieces, as shown in Diagram 2, so that upper curve is inside seam allowance of belly. Stitch along upper curve on each leg, then sew another line of stitches ¼" beneath first line. Pull legs straight up, and pin, keeping them away from seam allowances. Pin body pieces with right sides together, and stitch all around except for belly. Clip and turn.

Stuff body and each leg until plump or firm, as desired. Turn all open edges ⅜" to inside and slip-stitch closed.

**Finish:** Sew on button eyes. Wrap ribbon around neck and tie in a bow.

*Note: If your photocopier won't enlarge to 200%, enlarge image to 141%, and then enlarge resulting copy to 142%. To make a 400% enlargement, repeat process, starting with 200% copy.*

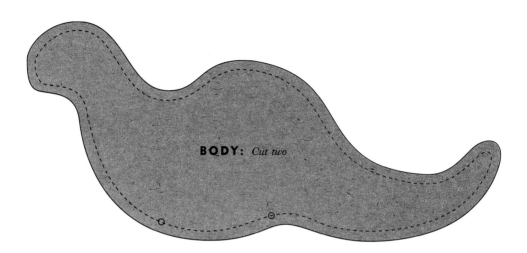

**BODY:** *Cut two*

**FRONT LEG:**
*Cut four*

**BACK LEG:**
*Cut four*

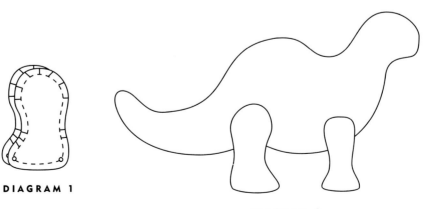

**DIAGRAM 1**

**DIAGRAM 2**

# *Light-Up* CAP

***Give a capful of Christmas fun to someone with a
bright mind and a sense of humor.***

**What You Will Need:**

1 plain baseball cap

1 set battery-operated miniature Christmas lights,
  such as Flora-Lite Co.'s product (see Sources)

Green and bronze acrylic paints in squeeze bottles
  with applicator tips

Gold puff paint

Craft knife #1

Pencil

Tracing paper

Straight pins

Scissors

Masking tape

**Painting Design:** Trace actual-size pattern onto
tracing paper and cut out. Pin to center front of
cap and trace around design lightly in pencil.
Using green paint, fill in tree shape. Apply paint
in curved strokes like boughs. Allow paint to dry

thoroughly before proceeding. Using bronze
paint, fill in tree trunk. Using gold puff paint,
add a gold star to treetop and make a dotted
gold garland. Let paint dry.

**Add Lights:** Using tip of craft knife, pierce
small holes in top and tips of tree
branches. Force miniature
lights through holes from
inside of hat. Inside cap,
secure wires and battery
pack in place with
masking tape.

**ACTUAL-SIZE PATTERN**

# SET FOR *Winter*

*Embellish this hat and gloves, then present them to your favorite little girl before Christmas, so she can show them off all through the Yuletide season.*

**What You Will Need:**

White knit hat

Pair of white knit gloves or mittens

9" × 12" piece green felt

1 yard red-and-white ribbon, ⅞" wide

1⅛ yards red satin cord, ¹⁄₁₆" wide

Brass-colored jingle bells: one ⅜", eleven ¼"

Small white feather boa

Green glitter paint

Glue gun, glue sticks, and tweezers, or sewing
   needle and thread in red, white, and green
   Pencil

Tracing paper

Small, flat paintbrush

Scissors

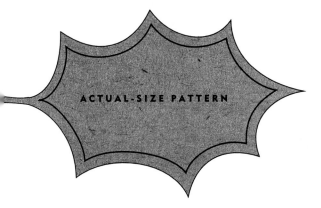

**ACTUAL-SIZE PATTERN**

**Cut:** Trace actual-size patterns for holly leaves onto tracing paper; cut out. Use patterns to cut 3 large leaves and 4 small leaves. Using brush, apply green glitter paint sparingly to one side of each leaf. Set aside to dry. Cut red-and-white ribbon into 3 equal pieces. Tie each into a bow, making loops 1" long on 2 bows, 1½" long on third. Trim streamer ends to desired length and cut an inverted V into each end. Cut red satin cord into 10 lengths varying between 3" and 5". Cut boa into one 3" length and two 1" lengths.

**Assemble:** Hot-glue elements carefully in place, referring to How to Use a Hot Glue Gun, on page 47, and using tweezers to avoid burning your fingers. Or tack items in place with a few small stitches using thread to match each individual element. Refer to photo for suggested positions. First, attach feather boa pieces: larger piece in a ring on one side of hat (here, on ribbing), each smaller piece to back of a glove, on ribbed cuff diagonally opposite thumb. Attach holly leaves so that they overlap boa piece, placing 3 larger leaves on hat, 2 small leaves on each glove. Center a bow on each group of holly leaves, putting bow with larger loops on hat. Tie a bell onto one end of each strand of satin cord, reserving 2 small bells. Divide strands to form 2 groups of 3, and 1 group of 4. For each group, hold opposite ends of strands together and knot. Push this knot into knot of ribbon bow, securing with glue or stitches. Hot-glue or sew remaining bells above bowknot on hat.

# Pine Tree TEA SET

*Hand-paint any surface that will not come into direct contact with food or beverages, either on this inviting tea set or a set of mugs.*

**What You Will Need:**

White china glazed ceramic tea set: teapot, sugar bowl, creamer

Red and green water-based glossy enamel paints, such as DEKA-Gloss from Decart, Inc. (see Sources)

Masking tape, ½" wide

2 disposable margarine tubs

Small piece of natural sea sponge

Flat ½" and fine, tapered paintbrushes

China marker or light-color crayon

**Paint Teapot:** Remove teapot lid. Place a strip of masking tape around spout, 1" from tip, and lengthwise along center of handle. Also use masking tape to make a diamond shape—a 3" square set on point—centered on 1 side of pot.

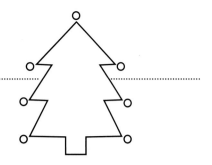

**ACTUAL-SIZE PATTERN**

Pour a generous amount of red paint into plastic tub. Practice sponge-painting on scrap paper: Dip sponge in paint, remove excess by pounding on newspaper, and apply to paper in up-and-down movement. Avoid overlapping areas already sponged. Sponge-paint teapot. Let paint set until dry to the touch, about 20 minutes. Remove tape, and let paint dry completely—another 40 minutes.

Place masking tape around inside of diamond shape to make a 2" square set on point. Trace or photocopy actual-size patterns. Cut out tree in center of teapot pattern to create stencil; omit ball ornaments. Center on diamond shape, and trace around inside of stencil using china marker or crayon. Remove pattern. Using green paint and fine tapered paintbrush, fill in tree; paint fine, feathery strokes along inside edges of masking tape to outline diamond shape; and create a pattern of dots and dashes along clean stripes on spout and handle. Using green paint and flat paintbrush, paint lid. Let paint dry thoroughly, then dot on red paint where indicated on pattern by open circles, and paint lid handle.

**Paint Sugar Bowl and Creamer:** Trace around smaller pattern. Following instructions for teapot, paint Christmas tree on center of one side of each. Then paint lid and side handles green. Let dry, then use red paint to paint rims and lid handle, and to make a row of dots along handles.

**Heat-Set:** Allow paint to dry at least 48 hours. Heat-set in oven, following manufacturer's instructions. These items should be washed in cool water with gentle detergents; they should not be left to soak in water, and should not be washed in a dishwasher.

**ACTUAL-SIZE PATTERN**

# Rocking COW

*Cow-abunga, Dudes! Anyone who loves country style will find these 4" ornaments udderly adorable for kitchen walls or doorknobs.*

**What You Will Need for Each Cow:**

Wood cow cut-out, 2¾"

Wood rocker, 4"

Small copper bell

White, black, green, red, and pink acrylic paints

Flat ½" and fine, tapered paintbrushes

Thick leather lace (sold with shoelaces) or round reed (sold with basketry supplies), 6" long

Glue gun and glue sticks

**Paint:** Using flat paintbrush, paint rocker red or green and paint cow white. Let paint dry completely. Referring to photo, pencil in details on cow. Use fine, tapered paintbrush to fill in areas.

**Glue Together:** Read How to Use a Hot Glue Gun, on page 47. Use hot glue to secure bell to cow's neck, attach rocker to cow's feet, and fix ends of lace or reed to back of cow, for a hanging loop.

# Cinnamon BEAR

*Decorate the outside of this 3½" bear or any clear, hollow ornament from a craft store and fill with a wonderful treat. To avoid spills, don't hang: use as stocking stuffer or tabletop decoration.*

**What You Will Need:**

1 clear glass or plastic hollow bear ornament, 3½" high

Red, pink, brown, and green acrylic paints

Cinnamon

Fine, tapered paintbrush

Wax paper

Tape

**Paint Outside:** Paint eyes and inside of ears brown, mouth and vest red, tie green, cheeks and vest buttons pink. Allow paint to dry completely.

**Fill Inside:** Remove hanger top or cap from ornament. To create a funnel, roll a sheet of wax paper, folded in half, into cone shape with a slight hole at the bottom; tape to secure. Use funnel to fill ornament with cinnamon. Replace hanger top.

# *Mini* CHRISTMAS TREE

*A festive 12" tree looks adorable peeking out of some-one's stocking on Christmas morning.*

**What You Will Need:**

Artificial fir tree with burlap-covered base,
    approximately 12" tall

2½ yards gold-edged, red-and-green ribbon, ⅛" wide

3 yards narrow red-and-green twisted cord or 1
    string of battery-operated miniature Christmas
    lights such as Flora-Lite Co.'s (see Sources)

Assorted miniatures for ornaments; shown here:

    12–14 tiny red bells

    14–16 tiny gold jingle bells

    10–12 miniature doves

    14–16 miniature glass ornaments

Glue gun and glue sticks

*Note: Read How to Use a Hot Glue Gun, page 47.*

**Prepare Ribbon:** Cut ⅛" ribbon into 6" lengths and tie each in a simple, pretty bow.

**Decorate Tree:** Wind miniature lights or twisted cord around tree, draping in a gracefully scalloped spiral from bottom to top. Using hot glue, attach ornaments and bows to boughs of tree. Reserve a special ornament or a multi-loop bow (see How to Make a Multi-Loop Bow, page 90) for top of tree. Work with one type of ornament or decoration at a time, and space items evenly all around.

# Teddy Bear TEA PARTY

*The perfect gift for a dollhouse lover: a 12"-high tableau that takes 'bearly' any effort to put together.*

**What You Will Need:**

Wooden framed window, 8⅜" × 11½", with windowbox, available at stores that sell dollhouse supplies

Stub wire (22–24 gauge)

⅛ yard cotton fabric

Small amount of raffia

Mini-wreath, 2"–3" in diameter

⅜ yard red-and-gold twisted cord, 1/16" wide

Few sprigs of preserved cedar

8 tea rosebuds

7–8 small pinecones

Sprigs red pepperberries

Sphagnum moss

Small bunch red everlastings

Miniature seated teddy bear

Miniature tea set

Red acrylic paint

Flat ¼" paintbrush

Pinking shears

Glue gun and gluesticks

Tweezers

*Note: Read How to Use a Hot Glue Gun, page 47, and How to Use Dried Florals, page 50.*

**Prepare Hanging Loops:** If tableau is to be hung, cut two 4" lengths of wire. Wrap each around top of window at a corner, and twist ends to make hanging loops.

**Cover Surfaces:** Paint window red. Allow to dry completely before proceeding. Cut fabric to fit around windowbox. Apply tacky glue along windowbox, and smooth fabric on top.

**Hang Curtains:** Cut two 8" × 9" rectangles with pinking shears, for curtain panels. Beginning at center top of window and working out to sides, pinch each panel into even pleats and hot-glue them in place. Use 1–2 strands of raffia as curtain ties. Secure sides of curtain in place with hot glue.

**Arrange Florals:** Use tweezers to hot-glue tiny items or moss, to avoid burning fingers. Hot-glue small sprigs of cedar to top of window, over curtains. Hot-glue pinecones to center of spray.

Wrap ribbon in a spiral around mini-wreath, securing ends with hot glue. Cover this join with a mini floral spray, hot-gluing cedar, pepperberries, and rosebuds. Hot-glue wreath to center of window. Fill windowbox with moss.

**Finish:** Arrange teddy and tea set, then secure in place with hot glue. Add a few stems of everlastings. It is a good idea to hot-glue lids to pots and sugar bowls, and teacups to their saucers.

> *"Let it snow,*
> *Let it snow,*
> *Let it snow"*

# *Tortoise Shell* BOXES

*Use the easiest technique ever to produce rich faux finishes on oval boxes, 7½"–15" long.*

**What You Will Need:**
Oval wood boxes with lids; shown here, a set
    of three: 7½" × 2", 10½" × 2¼", and 15" × 3"
Light oak and walnut wood stains
Moss green, teal, and dark red acrylic paints
Small piece of natural sea sponge
Flat ½" paintbrush
Plastic margarine tubs
Paper towels

**Create Tortoise Shell Finish:** Pour a generous
amount of walnut stain into plastic tub. Remove
box lids. Sponge all box and lid sides with walnut stain to create a mottled pattern. Allow to
dry completely before proceeding. When stain is
dry, pour light oak stain into another tub. Use a
paintbrush to apply stain heavily over lid and
box sides; let dry completely before proceeding.

**Add Flat Color Contrasts:** Paint top surfaces of
lids: small box—moss green; medium box—barn
red; large box—teal. Take care to keep paint on
top surface; if any paint gets on sides of lid, wipe
away immediately with a damp paper towel.

# *Candlestick* SNOWMEN

*Paint and decorate these nearly 6"-high candle taper holders with a frosty allure. Give them singly, in pairs, or in trios to melt someone's heart.*

**What You Will Need for Each Snowman:**
Wood snowman candlestick with hat, 5⅝" high,
    from Woodworks (see Sources)
White air-drying modeling compound
White, orange, and black acrylic paints
Small twigs
3 tiny jingle bells
⅜ yard ribbon, ¾" wide
⅛ yard ribbon, ½" wide
Small heart-shaped red button, yarn bow,
    or tiny silk flower, for hat trimming
Black fine, felt-tip marker
Small flat paintbrushes
Scissors
Glue gun and glue sticks

*Note: Read How to Use a Hot Glue Gun, page 47.*

**Sculpt Features:** With very small amount of
modeling compound, roll 2 tiny balls, for eyes,
and a small cone, for carrot nose. Let dry.

**Paint:** Paint body of snowman with white paint.
Let paint dry. Paint hat and eyes black. Paint
nose orange. When nose is dry, add small stripe
marks to carrot nose with black marker.

**Assemble:** Using hot glue, secure eyes and
carrot nose to face. Use marker to dot on a
smiling mouth beneath nose. Cut twigs to
two 2½" lengths and hot-glue one to each side
of snowman, for arms. Hot-glue bells, evenly
spaced, to body front, for buttons. For scarf,
cut a 10" length of ¾" ribbon. Using scissors,
fringe ends. Tie around snowman's neck and
secure with hot glue. Hot-glue ½" ribbon
around hat, for hat band, and cover ribbon
ends with tiny trimming.

# HOW TO
## *Wrap a Gift Box*

**What You Will Need:** A rectangular gift box, wrapping paper large enough to go around your box with a 1"–2" overlap and with an amount extending beyond each end that is more than long enough to meet at the center, paper cutting scissors, clear tape (double stick tape for best results).

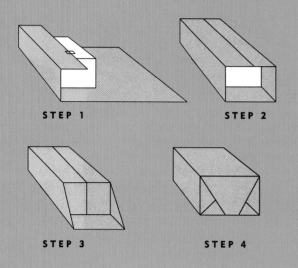

**STEP 1**   **STEP 2**

**STEP 3**   **STEP 4**

**Step 1:** Place the giftwrap wrong side up on a large, flat work surface. Center the box, upside down, on top. Bring one long edge of giftwrap to the center of the box and tape it in place at the center of the box bottom.

**Step 2:** Fold the opposite edge of the giftwrap ½" to the wrong side and crease. Bring this edge up to overlap the taped-down edge. Tape at the center to secure.

**Step 3:** At one end of the box, gently fold the paper from the bottom of the box down flat over the end of the box. Crease the triangles that form along each side of this surface.

**Step 4:** Fold each triangle in toward the other, flat onto the surface of the box end. This step will taper the remaining top flap into a triangle or trapezoid. Crease the folds that form and tape the side flaps if desired. Fold the point of the remaining flap to the wrong side so that it does not extend to the bottom surface of the box. Tape this flap in place. Repeat these steps to fold the giftwrap at the other end of the box.

# HOW TO
## *Wrap without Wrapping Paper*

Try these alternative methods for decorating your gift packages

❖ At newsstands, look for newspapers with foreign print, or financial newspapers that are printed on peach colored paper. Use red or gold ribbons for high contrast.

❖ Save the colored comic pages of Sunday newspapers over the course of a few months and you'll have all the giftwrap you'll need. Glue a little character or single frame of a comic strip to a solid-colored gift tag, to match.

❖ Purchase economical brown paper, or butcher paper. Sponge-paint, stencil, or rubber-stamp your giftwrap after it has covered the gift box. This way, you can center a few motifs on the box and you won't waste your efforts on areas of the giftwrap that won't show.

❖ Consider gift bags or boxes with the lid and box bottom wrapped separately. They're ecologically helpful because they're reusable.

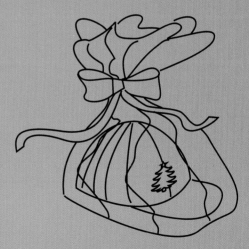

❖ No matter how oddly shaped your small or mid-sized gift is, you can wrap it in heavy cellophane. Available on rolls in both clear and colors, it adds sparkle and excitement but allows the recipient a peek at what's inside. Great for gifts you'll deliver and expect to be opened immediately. Center the gift on a large piece, bring the edges up and gather them together with ribbon or cord.

❖ Create an extraordinary gift by placing a few littler items in a basket. Use ribbons and bows strategically to decorate and to keep the items from spilling out. See the Card Caddy on page 14 for ways to dress up the basket.

❖ From the supermarket, aluminum foil, freezer wrap, colored cellophane wrap, brown lunch bags, and brown grocery bags all offer possibilities as wrapping paper, especially when combined with beautiful ribbons.

❖ Wrap gifts in tissue and nestle them into clear plastic containers from the bakery section of the supermarket. Use stickers to keep the package closed and to decorate it. Coordinate silver stars with dark tissue paper, sleds, skis, or skates with white tissue, or Santa stickers with green tissue.

❖ Use fabric to wrap a gift. Look for muslin, calico, or lining type fabrics on sale tables. Cut the edges with pinking shears, if available, and bring up the edges at the center top. Wrap and secure with a wired stem of silk ivy or holly. See the Pretty Pouches on page 53 for more ideas for embellishing your gift.

❖ Make a simple bag with burlap, available in colors as well as natural. Fold a rectangle in half, and sew along two adjacent sides. Fringe the top by pulling out threads along the raw edge. To close the bag, make a drawstring by guiding twine or yarn in a long running stitch all around the bag, close to the top.

❖ Paint a re-closable, empty, clean, cardboard box, covering up the commercial text and graphics. A 4" paint roller and some latex paint in a bright color could turn a cereal box, cylindrical oatmeal box, or box that once contained an assortment of chocolates into a great gift box. Apply some contrasting color dots, squiggles, lightning bolts, or personal message, using paint pens, and you've got a folk-art gift box that'll never get thrown away.

❖ Encase a gift in a big red bandanna, tying the corners together like the old stereotype of a hobo's traveling bag. Skip the stick, but poke a sprig of holly into the knot.

## HOW TO
# *Tie Up a Package*

Hold the ribbon 4–15 inches from the end (leaving a tail for a simple bow and streamer), and place on top of box where you want bow to be. Bring the ribbon around the length of the box, cross over the spot where you are holding the tail, and then wrap around the width of the box. Cut the ribbon off, leaving a similar tail at the opposite end. Bring this tail under the intersection of ribbons and tie to the opposite end in a knot. Use these tails to tie a simple bow, making a loop with each (see How to Tie a Simple Bow, below), or make a bow separately and use the streamer ends to tie it in place.

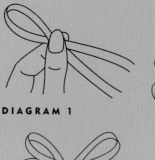

**DIAGRAM 1**

**DIAGRAM 2**

**DIAGRAM 3**

**DIAGRAM 4**

## HOW TO
# *Tie a Simple Bow*

Start about 9" from one end and leave that 9" tail unworked throughout. Make one loop whatever size you prefer—perhaps 2" long for small bows, 6" long for large bows. Hold the loop with your thumb and forefinger. See Diagram 1, below. Make another same-size loop right next to the first, and hold that with the thumb and forefinger of your other hand; see Diagram 2. Tie the two loops together. Diagram 3 shows the finished bow. Cut streamer ends on an angle, or notch wide ribbon ends with an inverted V shape.

## HOW TO
# *Make a Multi-Loop Bow*

Use at least 1¼ yards of ribbon (more for fuller bows), and a 5" strand of fine-or medium-gauge wire. Start, as for a simple bow, 9" from one end and leave that 9" tail unworked through the process. Make one loop the length you wish and hold it with your thumb and forefinger. See Diagram 1 above. Make a second, same-size loop in the opposite direction. Hold both loops in the center with thumb and forefinger. Make a third loop to one side of the first loop. See Diagram 2. Continue to make loops, alternating sides. Make a minimum of 3 loops on either side; however, the more loops you make, the fuller the bow will be. Wrap wire around the center of the loops. Hold the wire ends close to the ribbon, and twist the ribbon, rather than the wire, to secure tightly. See Diagram 3. Add another same-size loop at the center. Wrap the same wire around again, securing the last loop. See Diagram 4. Use the wire ends to attach the bow to the ribbon wrapping the gift box (or to anything else you wish to embellish with a bow). If desired, leave the ribbon ends long for streamers, but cut ends on an angle, or notch, as for a simple bow.

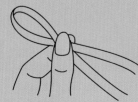

**DIAGRAM 1**

**DIAGRAM 2**

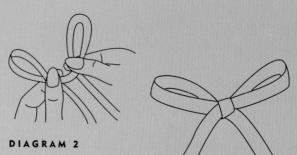

**DIAGRAM 3**

# HOW TO
## *Make a Pom-Pom Bow*

For a bow 6" in diameter, made with 20 loops, use 3½ yards of craft ribbon and a 5" strand of fine or medium-gauge wire. Starting at one end of ribbon, form a loop—6" long or as desired. Refer to Diagram 1 below. Wrap ribbon around the loop as many times as you want; each wrap will produce 2 loops. For a 20-loop bow, wrap ribbon around a total of 10 times. See Diagram 2. Flatten the loops and cut off little triangular notches at each end; take care not to cut too close to the center. See Diagram 3. Bring notched ends of the loop together to meet in the center, overlapping notches, as in Diagram 4. Wrap wire over the notched center. Holding the wire ends close to the ribbon, twist ribbon around for two or three rotations to secure wire tightly. Along one side of wire, pull out each loop, and twist it toward the center, alternating sides to create a full, half-sphere. See Diagram 5. Pull out the loops on the other side in the same way. Use the wire ends to attach the pompom bow at the intersection of ribbons on the gift box.

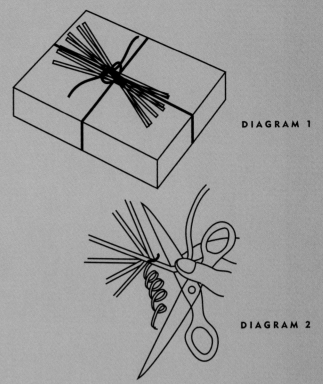

**DIAGRAM 1**

**DIAGRAM 2**

# HOW TO
## *Use Curling Ribbon*

Use curling ribbon to tie up a package, following directions on the opposite page, leaving 12" long tails. Cut several 24" strands of curling ribbon, in the same color or in as many colors as you wish. Lay them together with their centers at the knot. Use the 12" tails to wrap around the loose strands and tie tightly in a firm knot. See Diagram 1 above. Open wide the blades on a pair of scissors. Hold one ribbon strand close to the knot, and place it over one blade of the scissors. Hold the ribbon flat against the far side of the blade with your thumb, while you hold the knot with the thumb and forefinger of your other hand. Pull the scissors blade along the ribbon to the end. See Diagram 2. Ribbon will curl. Repeat with each ribbon end.

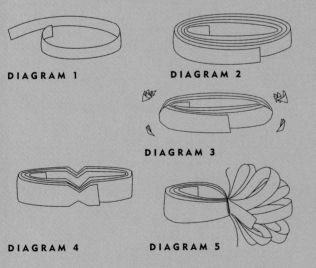

**DIAGRAM 1**

**DIAGRAM 2**

**DIAGRAM 3**

**DIAGRAM 4**

**DIAGRAM 5**

# Family Fun
## SOMETHING FOR EVERYONE

*Get the whole family into the holiday spirit by working on projects together.* ❖ *Turn the kitchen or play area into a workshop, keeping newspaper handy to protect the table and floor from paint, glue, and clay.* ❖ *We've selected incredibly easy projects, so that everyone from 3 to 103 can join in. No hot irons, glue guns, or ovens, and nothing to frustrate little ones—or even older ones, whose fingers may not be as nimble as they once were.* ❖ *Get a jump start on these projects with ready-mades and prepared kits. Look in your local craft store to find the kit for the Spool Dolly, the wood cut-outs for the Star-Power Elves, and plain stockings for you to embellish with paint and glitzy confetti.* ❖ *Now you're ready for the fun part of creativity.*

**ACTUAL-SIZE PATTERN**

# Star-Power ELVES

*Bet you can't make just one! Give each 2½" elf a slightly different look. Add hanging loops or a dowel to ring these little stars around a tree, a wreath, a napkin ring, or a plant stick.*

**What You Will Need for Each Elf:**

Wood star shape, 2½" wide

Red, green, and black acrylic paints

Flat and fine, tapered paintbrushes

Choice of 1 trimming: rhinestones, 1 each red
    and green; 4 tiny pompons; sequins, four 3 mm
    or two 5 mm; or tiniest jingle bell

White craft glue with applicator tip

Masking tape, ¾" wide

**Paint Star:** Place wood star on table protected with newspaper. See photo and actual-size pattern for suggestions on painting and decorating each elf. Cover up areas that do not get painted: From masking tape, cut out 2 circles, ⅝" in diameter. Stick 1 on star under the top point, for face. Cut other tape circle in half, and stick a semi-circle over each "hand." Use flat paintbrush and red or green paint to paint over front surface of wood star. Let dry, paint back, let dry, then remove tape.

**Add Details:** Using tapered paintbrush and a contrasting paint color, paint a curved line along top of face, for hat rim; a thin band ¼" from points on each outstretched "arm," for cuffs; and 2 bottom points of star, for shoes. For face, dot on 2 red cheeks and 2 black eyes as shown. Glue on trimmings; see the photo for ideas.

# Pompon WREATH

*This cheerful ornament—4½" in diameter—is just perfect to hang on a tree, a doorknob, or a wall.*

**What You Will Need:**

Mini twig wreath, 3" in diameter

About 75 green pompons

15 tiny red pompons

12" strand of red yarn

White craft glue with applicator tip

**Make Hanging Loop:** Push yarn through a strong section of twig wreath. Pull yarn ends even with each other and tie a knot 2" away from wreath. Pull loop so that knot is against wreath, and make a bow on the knot, using ends of yarn.

**Make Wreath:** Place twig wreath on a table protected with newspaper. Turn wreath so that bow is on underside, at center of top. Glue green pompons to twig wreath, covering front and side edges completely. Let glue dry, then glue tiny red pompons, in groups of 3, on top. See photo.

# Candy-Mold
## ORNAMENTS

*Make 2–4" ornaments that look good enough to eat. Because air-drying modeling compound is non-toxic, you can still use the same clay mold later for cookies or candies.*

**What You Will Need:**

Clay cookie molds; shown here: Santa Bear shape, sheep shape

Package of white air-drying modeling compound

Acrylic paints in assorted colors

Red and green tinsel and plush pipe cleaners

Small jingle bells

Wood craft stick (Popsicle stick) or blunt knife

Small flat and thin, tapered paintbrushes

Black fine-line permanent-ink marking pen

**Make Molds:** Press modeling compound into cookie mold and pat into place with fingertips. Let dry for about 3 days, or until no longer cool or damp to the touch. Use a craft stick or blunt knife to carefully peel clay from mold, beginning at one edge.

**Paint:** If paints are thick, thin them by mixing in a small amount of water. Use flat brush and acrylic paint to paint ornaments. Let first color of paint dry before painting second color next to it. After paint is dry, add any small details (such as eyes, nose, and mouth) with marker or thin, tapered brush.

**Trim and Hang:** Thread bells on a pipe cleaner and twist around necks or elsewhere on shape. Form hanging loops by twisting ends of another pipe cleaner onto back of first pipe cleaner.

# Glitter-Berry
## STOCKING

*A little shimmer from metallic confetti puts the kick into this 8" stocking!*

**What You Will Need:**

Ready-made plain canvas stocking, 8" high, available from the Dalee Book Co. (see Sources)

Green acrylic paint

Package of metallic red and purple heart-shaped confetti

Small paintbrush

White craft glue

**Create Berries:** With glue, paint 6 groups of 3 large dots, well spaced, over front of stocking. Cover dots with heart confetti, for holly berries. Let dry.

**Paint Holly Leaves:** Paint green leaves freehand: Make little strokes around each group of berries, as shown in photo. Let dry.

*"So hang your stocking*

*And say your prayers,*

*'Cause Santa Claus*

*comes tonight."*

# *Spool* TREE

*To build this colorful 3½"-high ornament, look for little empty wood spools in the wood section of your local craft store.*

## What You Will Need:

12 wood spools, ⅝" high

6-strand embroidery floss: 2 skeins bright green, 1 skein brown or sepia

½" star button

6 small jingle bells

Bright red and brown acrylic paints

Small flat paintbrush

Scissors

White craft glue

**DIAGRAM 1**

**Prepare Spools:** Paint 11 spools red. Paint last remaining spool brown. Let spools dry completely.

Wind green floss around the 11 red spools to cover them well. Glue floss at beginning (see Diagram 1) and at end. Wind brown floss on remaining spool, gluing in the same way.

**Make Tree:** Position red spools so that they form a pyramid (see Diagram 2). Glue together in rows. When glue is dry, glue the brown spool at bottom center, for tree trunk.

**Decorate Tree:** Glue one arm of six-pointed star button in hole of top spool; glue a loop of floss behind star, for hanging finished ornament. Or, thread floss ends through shank of button and into hole of top spool. Glue jingle bells between spools as shown in photo and Diagram 3.

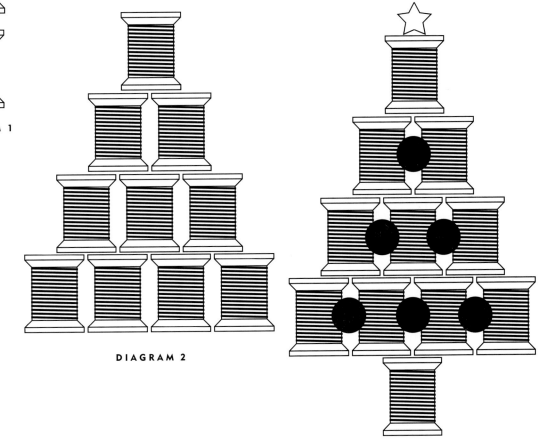

**DIAGRAM 2**

**DIAGRAM 3**

# *Spool* DOLLY

*Give this 5" spool doll, assembled from a kit, eyes and hair to match those of someone in your family and clothes to match your home.*

**What You Will Need:**

Kit for 5"-tall spool doll (see note below)

½ yard printed ribbon, 3" wide, for clothing

½ yard satin ribbon, ⅛" wide

4 black seed beads (optional for dress buttons)

Blue and red fine-tip, permanent-ink markers

Embroidery floss or pearl cotton in color to match wide ribbon and as desired, for hair

Tacky glue

Scissors

Large-eyed needle

**DIAGRAM FOR DOLL CONSTRUCTION**

**Assemble Doll:** Follow the kit instructions to assemble spool doll. *Note:* If you cannot locate a kit, use wood spools, wood beads, and twine or household string to assemble doll according to our construction diagram. Tie twine to top of head for hanging doll as an ornament.

Use markers to draw on a face. Glue floss to doll's head and arrange hair as you wish, but keep twine hanging loop free.

**Add Clothing:** From printed ribbon, cut an 11" length for dress and a 3" length for scarf. For dress, fold 11" piece crosswise in half, with right sides together. Glue short edges together to form a ring, and let glue dry. Turn fabric ring right side out. Flatten ring so that joined edges are at center of back. Cut ¾" slits in sides, ¼" from edge. With needle and floss or pearl cotton, sew a running stitch ¼" from one long edge (top). Pull floss ends to gather the stitches. Place on doll and pull arms through the slits, then pull floss ends to gather edge tightly at neck.

For triangular scarf, cut a 1¾" square from wide ribbon and fold diagonally in half, with wrong sides together. Glue edges so it stays folded. Cut ⅛" ribbon in half, and glue 1 piece to each side of triangle, for scarf ties. Cut a tiny hole in top of scarf and draw twine hanging loop through it. Wrap scarf around dolly's head and tie ribbons together in a bow.

# *Gingerbread* ANGELS

*Though they're not for eating, these 5″-high cookie-like paper dolls make heavenly garlands, Christmas cards, or ornaments for your tree or window.*

**What You Will Need:**

Sheet of brown construction paper

White, red, green, and black acrylic paints in squeeze
   bottles with applicator tips

Pencil

Tracing paper

Scissors

**Cut Shapes:** Trace actual-size angel pattern onto tracing paper, or photocopy. Cut out. Place pattern on construction paper, with 1 angel hand against the edge. See Diagram 1. Trace around pattern. At tip of other hand, begin folding paper like an accordion; see Diagram 2. Hold folded edges together firmly and cut out angel through all layers. Be careful not to cut the wing tips, hands, and skirt bottoms where they meet the edges. Unfold angel chain. Place pattern on remaining areas of construction paper to cut out single angels.

**Paint:** Practice using squeeze bottles to paint even dots. See photo for suggested design of dots. Decorate angels with dots of paint. Let paint dry completely before handling angels.

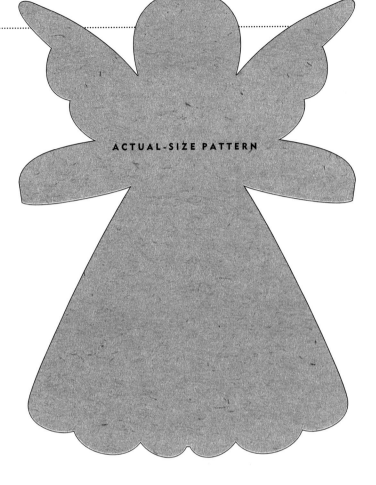

**ACTUAL-SIZE PATTERN**

**DIAGRAM 1**

**DIAGRAM 2**

# Gingerbread Boys ON THE RUN

*If you can't chase down this cookie cutter, slightly bend the clay feet of a classic gingerbread man shape and watch him run. Make a big batch of these 5" ornaments—but remember: they're not for eating!*

**What You Will Need:**

Running gingerbread boy cookie cutter

White air-dry modeling compound

Brown acrylic paint

Black acrylic paint in squeeze bottle with
   applicator tip

String, pearl cotton, or dental floss, for hanging loop

Small flat paintbrush

Wax paper

Rolling pin

Wood skewer

**Cut Shapes:** On a flat surface, roll modeling compound out to about 3⁄16" thickness on wax paper using a rolling pin. Use cookie cutter to cut out as many shapes as can fit. Place shapes on clean wax paper on a flat surface. If ornaments are to be hung, use a skewer to pierce a hole in top of head or end of one arm. Let dry for 2–3 days, or until modeling compound is no longer cool and damp to the touch.

**Paint:** Paint each body brown. Let dry. Squeeze bottle of black paint to make small, raised dots for eyes, smiling mouth, and buttons.

**Hang:** When dry, thread string through hole and tie ends for hanging loop.

# Delectable Gifts

## A TASTE OF HOLIDAY CHEER

*A gift of food during the holidays can be a delicious treat for someone dear to you.* ❖ *Preparing festive fare is also practical, as friends and relatives have a tendency to drop by unexpectedly at this time of year. Be sure to have plenty of tempting cookies and savory breads to offer your cherished guests.* ❖ *Many of the recipes included here can be made ahead and stored or frozen, so you don't have to wait until the hectic holidays are upon you.* ❖ *And don't forget to cook up extra batches of these tasty recipes to keep enough for you and your family to enjoy!*

## FRUIT-FLAVORED *Vinegar*

*Add a refreshing zing to salads and a variety of other recipes with this tasty condiment.*

1 cup pitted tart red cherries or blueberries
2 cups white wine vinegar

In a small stainless-steel or enamel saucepan combine fruit and vinegar. Bring to a boil; reduce heat. Boil gently, uncovered, for 3 minutes. Remove from heat and cover loosely with cheesecloth; cool.

Pour mixture into a clean 1-quart jar. Cover jar tightly with a nonmetallic lid (or cover with plastic wrap and then seal tightly with a metal lid). Let stand in a cool, dark place for 2 weeks.

Line a colander with several layers of 100% cotton cheesecloth. Strain vinegar mixture through the colander and let it drain into a bowl. Discard fruit. Transfer strained vinegar to a clean 1-pint glass jar or bottle. If desired, add a few additional pieces of fresh fruit to the jar or bottle. Cover jar or bottle tightly with a nonmetallic lid (or cover with plastic wrap and then seal tightly with a metal lid). Store vinegar in a cool, dark place for up to 6 months. Makes about 1½ cups (24 tablespoon-size servings)

## *Fiery* MARINATED OLIVES

*These olives will wake up your tastebuds, but keep them refrigerated because they are not processed after marinating.*

2 3-ounce jars almond-stuffed olives, drained
⅓ cup salad oil
¼ cup water
3 tablespoons lime juice
1 tablespoon snipped cilantro
1 tablespoon crushed red pepper
1 teaspoon cumin seed
1 clove garlic, minced

In a small saucepan combine all ingredients. Bring to a boil; reduce heat. Simmer, covered, 5 minutes. Remove from heat. Cool to room temperature.

Use a slotted spoon to transfer olives to jars with tight-fitting lids. Pour cooking liquid over olives in jars. Cover and chill in refrigerator 4–7 days before serving. Store in refrigerator up to 3 weeks. Makes about 2 cups.

## *Western* PEPPER JELLY

*Spoon this spunky jelly atop cornbread muffins, or brush over chicken while roasting to add some kick.*

2 medium cooking apples (such as Granny Smith or Jonathan), cored and coarsely chopped
1 medium green sweet pepper, seeded and coarsely chopped
6–8 jalapeño peppers, halved
1½ cups cider vinegar
5 cups sugar
¼ cup water
½ of 6-ounce package liquid fruit pectin (1 foil pouch)
¼ cup finely chopped green sweet pepper
¼ cup finely chopped red sweet pepper
1 small banana pepper, finely chopped

In a 4- or 5-quart Dutch oven, combine apples, the coarsely chopped green pepper, jalapeño peppers, vinegar, sugar, and ¼ cup water. Bring to a boil; reduce heat. Boil gently, uncovered, for 10 minutes. Strain mixture through a sieve, pressing with the back of a spoon to remove all liquid (should have 4 cups). Discard pulp.

Return liquid to Dutch oven; bring to a boil. Add pectin; return to boiling. Boil hard for 1 minute, stirring constantly. Remove from heat. Stir in the finely chopped red and green sweet peppers and the banana pepper.

Pour into hot, sterilized half-pint canning jars (which have been sterilized by boiling for 10 minutes). Leave ¼" headspace. Wipe rims; adjust lids. Process in boiling-water bath for 5 minutes (start timing after water boils). Remove from water bath; cool on wire rack until set (jelly will take 2–3 days to set). Makes about 5 half-pints.

Note: Chopped pepper pieces will float to top on standing.

# *Gingered* PEAR RELISH

*Put some spark into any pork or ham dinner with this flavorful sweet and savory relish.*

5 cups firm, ripe pear, peeled, cored, and diced
  (3 pounds)
2½ cups chopped onion
2 cups chopped red sweet pepper
1 cup cider vinegar
1 cup sugar
2 tablespoons Dijon-style mustard
1 tablespoon grated ginger root
1 teaspoon mustard seed
1 teaspoon celery seed
½ teaspoon bottled hot pepper sauce

Bring ingredients to boiling in a Dutch oven; reduce heat. Boil gently, uncovered, 45 minutes or until slightly thickened; stir often. Remove from heat.

Ladle into hot, clean half-pint canning jars, leaving ¼" headspace. Wipe rims; adjust lids. Process in boiling-water bath for 15 minutes (start timing after water boils). Makes 6 half-pints.

# *Pineapple* MARMALADE

*Here's a tangy twist on an old breakfast favorite.*
*It's a welcome addition to any table.*

2 large oranges

2 large lemons

1 cup unsweetened pineapple juice

1 20-ounce can crushed pineapple (juice pack)

1 1¾-ounce package regular powdered fruit pectin

5 cups sugar

Score citrus peels into 4 lengthwise sections. Remove peels with a vegetable peeler. Cut into very thin strips. In a medium saucepan combine peels and pineapple juice. Bring to a boil. Cover and simmer 20 minutes; do not drain.

Cut white membrane off fruit. Section fruit over a bowl to catch juices. Discard seeds. Add fruits and juices to peel mixture. Simmer, covered, 10 minutes more. Add undrained pineapple.

Transfer fruit mixture to an 8-quart Dutch oven; stir in pectin. Bring to full rolling boil, stirring constantly. Stir in sugar; return to full rolling boil. Boil hard 1 minute, stirring constantly. Remove from heat; quickly skim off foam.

Ladle at once into hot, clean half-pint canning jars, leaving ¼" headspace. Wipe rims; adjust lids. Process in boiling-water bath 15 minutes (start timing after water boils). Makes 7 half-pints.

*"And God bless you and send you*

*A Happy New Year,*

*And God send you*

*A Happy New Year."*

# *Banana* GINGERBREAD

*Serve this yummy bread with tea or hot cider when friends stop by on a holiday afternoon.*

2¼ cups all-purpose flour

½ cup sugar

1½–2 teaspoons ground ginger

1 teaspoon baking powder

1 teaspoon ground cinnamon

½ teaspoon baking soda

¼ teaspoon salt

1 cup mashed ripe banana (2 to 3 medium bananas)

½ cup butter-flavored shortening or margarine

½ cup molasses

3 eggs

½ cup chopped walnuts or almonds

Grease three 5½" × 3" × 2" loaf pans; set aside.

In a large mixing bowl combine 1 cup of the flour with the sugar, ginger, baking powder, cinnamon, baking soda, and salt. Add mashed banana, shortening or margarine, and molasses. Beat with an electric mixer on low speed till blended, then on high speed for 2 minutes. Add remaining flour and the eggs; beat until blended. Stir in nuts.

Pour batter into the prepared pans. Bake in a 350° oven for 40 minutes or until a toothpick inserted near the center comes out clean. Cool for 10 minutes on a wire rack. Remove from the pan; cool thoroughly on a wire rack. Makes 3 small loaves (6 slices each).

# *Golden* FRUIT CONSERVE

*With its golden color and taste, this wonderful conserve will light up any holiday breakfast table.*

1¾ pounds nectarines (about 5)

1½ pounds apricots (about 15) or 1¼ pounds
    peaches (about 4)

1 cup light raisins

2 tablespoons lemon juice

5½ cups sugar

1 1¾-ounce package regular powdered fruit pectin

½ teaspoon margarine or butter

1 cup sliced almonds

Peel, pit, and coarsely chop nectarines and apricots or peaches separately; mash both fruits (should have 2¼ cups nectarine mixture and 2 cups apricot). In an 8- or 10-quart kettle or Dutch oven, combine the mashed fruit, raisins, and lemon juice. Place sugar into a bowl; set aside.

Add the pectin and margarine to the fruit mixture; bring to a full rolling boil over high heat, stirring constantly with a wooden spoon. Add sugar quickly. Return to a full rolling boil, stirring constantly. Boil hard for 1 minute, stirring constantly. Remove from heat; skim off any foam with a metal spoon. Stir in the almonds.

Ladle mixture into hot, clean half-pint canning jars, leaving ¼" headspace. Wipe rims; adjust lids. Process in boiling-water bath for 15 minutes (start timing after water boils). Makes 8 half-pints.

## QUICK BREAD LOAVES

Freeze quick bread loaves after they have been baked and cooled. Wrap them tightly in heavy foil or place in freezer bags and seal. Freeze for up to 3 months.

For a special gift, wrap a quick bread loaf in plastic wrap and place on a small cutting board. Then wrap both loaf and board with colored cellophane and add a perky bow to the handle. If desired, cut the gift tag in the shape of a bread slice and tie it to the bow.

# Pear ZUCCHINI BREAD

*Surprise your teatime or dinner guests with this unusual bread. They'll want to know the recipe too!*

Nonstick spray coating
2 cups all-purpose flour
1 cup rye flour
2 teaspoons pumpkin pie spice
1 teaspoon baking soda
½ teaspoon baking powder
½ teaspoon salt
2 cups chopped, peeled pears or one 16-ounce
   can pear halves, drained and chopped
1 cup granulated sugar
1 cup packed brown sugar
1 cup finely shredded, unpeeled zucchini
1 cup cooking oil
3 eggs
1 tablespoon vanilla
½ cup chopped pecans

Spray two 8" × 4" × 2" loaf pans with nonstick coating; set aside.

In a medium mixing bowl combine flours, pumpkin pie spice, baking soda, baking powder, and salt.

In a large mixing bowl combine pears, sugars, zucchini, oil, eggs, and vanilla; mix well. Add flour mixture; stir just until combined. Stir in chopped nuts.

Pour batter into prepared pans. Bake in a 350° oven for 55–60 minutes or until a toothpick inserted near the center comes out clean. Cool for 10 minutes on a wire rack. Remove bread from pan; cool thoroughly on rack. Wrap in plastic wrap and store overnight before slicing. Makes 2 loaves (16 slices each).

# Peach JAM

*Full of homemade comfort, this mellow jam will start everyone's day off right.*

3 pounds ripe peaches (10–12)
2 tablespoons lemon juice
1 1¾-ounce package lite powdered fruit pectin*
3½ cup sugar
½ teaspoon margarine or butter

Set rack in canner; fill half full with water. Cover; heat over high heat. Also heat a teakettle or large panful of additional water.

Meanwhile, wash and rinse 6–7 half-pint canning jars thoroughly. Pour boiling water over jars and let stand in hot water until needed. Prepare lids according to manufacturer's directions.

For easy peeling, immerse peaches in boiling water for 20–30 seconds or until skins start to crack; remove peaches and plunge into cold water. Peel, pit, and finely chop peaches; measure 5 cups. In an 8- or 10-quart kettle, combine peaches and lemon juice. Combine pectin and ¼ cup of the sugar; stir into peach mixture. Add margarine or butter (this reduces foaming during cooking).

Bring peach mixture to a full rolling boil, stirring constantly. Stir in the remaining 3¼ cups sugar. Return to a full rolling boil. Boil hard 1 minute, stirring constantly. Remove from heat. With a large metal spoon, quickly skim off any foam.

Ladle jam at once into the hot, clean half-pint canning jars, leaving ¼" headspace between jam and rims. Wipe jar rims clean with a damp towel. Top with lids and screw-on bands, following manufacturer's directions.

When water in canner is hot, place jars on rack using a jar lifter. When all jars are in, fill canner with more boiling water to about 1" over jar tops. Cover, and heat to a brisk, rolling boil (when boiling, start counting processing time).

Process in boiling-water bath for 15 minutes. During processing, keep the water boiling gently; add more boiling water if the water level drops. If water stops boiling when you add more, stop counting the time, turn up the heat, and wait for a full boil before continuing to count. At end of processing time, turn off heat; remove jars. Cool on rack.

When jam is completely cool, check jar seals by pressing center of each lid. If dip in lid holds, the jar is sealed. Label jars. Store sealed jars in a cool, dry place and use within 1 year. Store unsealed jam (the dip in the lid did not hold) in refrigerator or freezer. Makes 6–7 half-pints.

*Note:* Use only lite powdered fruit pectin for this recipe. The recipe amounts are designed for this product and do not work with other pectin products.

# *Holiday* TEA RING

*Candied fruits and nuts sparked with a rum-flavored topping give this tea ring true Christmas spirit.*

4¼–4¾ cups all-purpose flour
1 package active dry yeast
1 cup milk
½ cup margarine or butter
1 cup sugar
¾ teaspoon salt
3 eggs
⅓ cup margarine or butter, melted
½ cup candied red cherries, chopped*
½ cup candied green cherries, chopped*
½ cup candied pineapple, chopped*
½ cup chopped pecans
Rum Icing (see below)

In a large mixing bowl stir together 2 cups of the flour and the yeast.

In a medium saucepan heat the milk, the ½ cup margarine or butter, ½ cup of the sugar, and the salt until warm (120°–130°). Add the milk mixture and the eggs to the flour mixture. Beat with an electric mixer on low speed for 30 seconds, scraping the sides of the bowl. Beat on high speed for 3 minutes. Stir in as much of the remaining flour as you can.

Cover and refrigerate the dough for 6–24 hours. Stir down dough. Grease 3 pans, using either 9"

pie plates, 8 × 1½" round baking pans, or 9 × 1½" round baking pans; set aside.

Divide the dough into 3 portions. On a lightly floured surface, roll 1 portion into a rectangle, about 14" × 8". Brush the rectangle of dough with one-third of the melted margarine or butter. Sprinkle rectangle with one-third of the remaining ½ cup sugar. Sprinkle with one-third of the candied cherries, the candied pineapple, and the nuts.

Roll rectangle of dough loosely, starting from a long side; pinch edges together. Shape the roll into a circle, pinching the ends together. Place the circle of dough in a prepared pie plate or in a baking pan. Using scissors, cut from the outer edge almost through to the center at 1" intervals; twist each 1" piece ½ turn to the left to form a tea ring. Repeat with the 2 remaining portions of dough to make 2 more tea rings.

Cover lightly with plastic wrap; allow the dough to rise for 6–24 hours in the refrigerator. Bake tea rings in a 375° oven for about 20 minutes or until light brown. Transfer to a wire rack. Brush tea rings with Rum Icing while hot. Serve tea rings warm or at room temperature. (To freeze, wrap the cooled tea rings thoroughly in freezer wrap; seal, label, and freeze. Store tea rings for up to 3 months in the freezer. To serve, thaw tea rings overnight at room temperature.) Makes 3 tea rings (8 servings each).

*Note:* You may substitute 1½ cups of diced mixed candied fruits and peels for the candied cherries and candied pineapple.

**Rum Icing**
In a mixing bowl stir together 1 cup sifted powdered sugar, ¼ teaspoon rum extract, and enough hot water (about 1–2 tablespoons) to make of icing consistency.

# *Christmas* CUTOUTS

*One of the best-loved traditions of Christmas, baking cutout cookies will bring the taste—and smell—of happy holidays into your home.*

¾ cup butter

2½ cups all-purpose flour

1 cup sugar

2 eggs

1 teaspoon baking powder

1 teaspoon vanilla

Beat butter in mixing bowl with electric mixer on medium to high speed 30 seconds or until softened. Add half the flour, the sugar, eggs, baking powder, and vanilla. Beat until thoroughly combined. Beat or stir in remaining flour. Divide dough in half. Cover; chill for 1–2 hours or until easy to handle.

Roll each portion on a lightly floured surface to about ⅛" thickness. Cut into desired shapes. Place 1" apart on ungreased cookie sheet.

Bake in a 375° oven for 7–8 minutes or until edges are firm and bottoms are very lightly browned. Remove cookies and cool on a wire rack. Decorate, if desired. Makes about 8 dozen.

## COOKIE ORNAMENTS

Turning Christmas cutout cookies into tree ornaments is simple. Before you bake them, use a drinking straw to poke a hole at the top end of each cookie. If after baking you notice that the holes have sealed up too much to allow a string or ribbon to pass through, make the holes again while the cookies are still soft. Then, after the cookies are completely cooled and decorated, run ribbon, yarn, or thread through the holes in the cookies. Tie at the top, forming a large loop for hanging on a tree branch.

# YULE *Dollies*

1 recipe Chrismas Cutouts

Victorian paper scraps

2 cups sifted powdered sugar

Milk

Prepare dough for Christmas Cutouts as directed. Place paper scrap on dough; cut around paper, allowing ¼" margin. Remove paper; transfer cookies to ungreased baking sheet.

Bake in 375° oven for 7–8 minutes. Remove cookies and cool on wire rack.

Mix powdered sugar and enough milk in bowl to make of piping consistency. Use small amount of icing to attach the paper scraps to the appropriate cookies.

# SEED *Cakes*

1 recipe Christmas Cutouts

4 teaspoons sesame seed or 1 tablespoon caraway seed

Milk

Sesame seed (optional)

Prepare dough for Christmas Cutouts as directed, except substitute sesame or caraway seed for vanilla. Divide the dough and chill as directed.

Roll each half of dough into a 12" × 10" rectangle. Cut into 2" squares or circles using a knife or scalloped cutter. Place on ungreased cookie sheet. Brush with milk. Sprinkle sesame cakes with additional sesame seed, if desired. Bake and cool as directed. Makes 60.

## FROTHY MIDNIGHT *Mocha*

*Sitting by a fire, cuddled up in a blanket, who wouldn't love a cup of this heartwarming mocha?*

2½ cups nonfat dry milk powder
1 cup sifted powdered sugar
½ cup unsweetened cocoa powder
¼ cup instant coffee crystals
½ teaspoon apple pie spice

To make mocha mix, in a 1-quart airtight storage container combine milk powder, powdered sugar, cocoa powder, coffee crystals, and apple pie spice. Cover and shake well to mix. Makes 10 (6-ounce) servings.

To make a cup of mocha, first stir the mix. Place ⅓ cup of the mix in a blender container or food processor. Cover. With blender or processor running, add ⅔ cup boiling water through opening in lid or center feed tube. Blend or process until mixed and frothy.

---

## COOKIE GIFTS

Simple gift containers for cookies include ribbon-tied paper sacks, decorated coffee cans, wide-mouth canning jars covered with fabric-trimmed lids, cellophane-lined baskets, handsome cardboard containers made just for gift-giving, paper plates covered with plastic wrap and trimmed with a bow, and decorative cookie tins.

Regardless of the container, be sure the cookies are well protected from air and moisture. For containers that do not have tight-fitting lids, wrap the cookies in plastic wrap or seal in a plastic bag before placing them in the container.

---

## CHERRY-CHOCOLATE *Drops*

*Two great flavors—cherry and chocolate—make these cookies a popular holiday treat.*

1 cup margarine or butter
¾ cup packed brown sugar
2 egg yolks
2 ounces semisweet chocolate, melted and cooled
1½ teaspoons finely shredded orange peel
1 teaspoon ground cinnamon
1 teaspoon vanilla
¼ teaspoon salt
2¼ cups all-purpose flour
1½–2 cups finely chopped pecans
2 egg whites
¾ cup cherry jelly or preserves

In large mixing bowl beat margarine or butter and brown sugar with an electric mixer on medium speed for 30 seconds. Add egg yolks, beating well. Blend in melted chocolate, orange peel, cinnamon, vanilla, and salt. Stir in flour.

Place pecans and egg whites in 2 separate small, shallow bowls. Slightly beat egg whites with a fork. Shape dough into 1" balls. Dip each ball into egg white; roll in pecans to coat.

Place balls, 2" apart, on lightly greased baking sheets. Using your thumb, make slight a indentation in top of each cookie. Bake in 350° oven about 12 minutes or until edges are firm. Cool cookies on a wire rack. Fill centers of cooled cookies with a small spoonful of jelly or preserves. Makes about 60 cookies.

# *Classic* GINGERBREAD COOKIES

*Capture the flavor of an old-fashioned Christmas with these well-loved mouthwatering munchies.*

½ cup shortening
2½ cups all-purpose flour
½ cup sugar
½ cup molasses
1 egg
1 tablespoon vinegar
1 teaspoon baking powder
1 teaspoon ground ginger
½ teaspoon baking soda
½ teaspoon ground cinnamon
½ teaspoon ground cloves
Powdered Sugar Icing (optional; see below)
Decorative candies (optional)

In a mixing bowl beat the shortening with an electric mixer on medium to high speed for 30 seconds. Add about half of the flour. Then add the sugar, molasses, egg, vinegar, baking powder, ginger, baking soda, cinnamon, and cloves. Beat until combined, scraping bowl occasionally. Beat or stir in remaining flour. Cover and chill about 3 hours or until dough is easy to handle.

Divide chilled dough in half. On a lightly floured surface, roll each half of the dough to ⅛" thickness. Using 2½" cookie cutters, cut dough into desired shapes. Place 1" apart on greased cookie sheets.

Bake in a 375° oven for 5–6 minutes or until edges are lightly browned. Cool on cookie sheets for 1 minute. Remove cookies and cool on wire racks. If desired, prepare Powdered Sugar Icing. Decorate cookies with icing and, if desired, decorative candles. Makes about 36 cookies.

**Powdered Sugar Icing**
In a small mixing bowl stir together 1 cup sifted powdered sugar, ¼ teaspoon vanilla, and enough milk (1–2 tablespoons) to make icing of drizzling consistency.

## MAILING COOKIES

When sending cookies by mail, be sure to select good travelers. These include most bar cookies and drop cookies as well as slice-and-bake cookies. Avoid frosted and filled cookies; the filling or frosting can soften, causing the cookies to stick to each other or to the wrappings. Cutout cookies with delicate edges also can break during shipping. If you want to send cutouts, select those with compact or rounded shapes, such as bells or snowmen, rather than those with points or narrow pieces.

Use a heavy box lined with plastic or foil. Then cushion the cookies with filler such as plastic bubble wrap, foam packing pieces, or crumpled tissue paper, paper towels, or waxed paper.

Wrap the cookies in plastic wrap, individually or two at a time, back to back. Place them in the packing box with layers of filler in between cookie layers. Make sure the box is full enough that the contents will not shift when it is closed. If desired, pack cookies in a decorative cookie tin, then pack container in a shipping box.

Remember to include the addresses of both sender and receiver inside the box, just in case the box is accidentally torn open. Seal the box closed with strapping tape. Add an address and apply transparent tape over the address to prevent it from becoming smeared during handling. Mark the box "Perishable."

# *Eggnog* BREAD

*What better way to give quick bread a Christmas twist than with the warm, rich flavor of eggnog?*

4¾ cups all-purpose flour

¾ cup sugar

4 teaspoons baking powder

½ teaspoon salt

½ teaspoon ground nutmeg

2 beaten eggs

2¾ cups canned or dairy eggnog

½ cup cooking oil

¾ cup chopped pecans

¾ cup snipped dried apricots

Eggnog Icing (see below)

Stir together flour, sugar, baking powder, salt, and nutmeg in a large mixing bowl. Combine eggs, eggnog, and oil; add to the dry ingredients, stirring just until combined. Stir in chopped pecans and snipped apricots.

Turn into two greased 8" × 4" × 2" loaf pans. Bake in a 350° oven for 55–60 minutes or until a toothpick inserted near center comes out clean. (Cover with foil after 40 minutes if the bread browns too quickly.)

Cool in pan for 10 minutes. Remove bread from pan; cool on wire rack. Wrap bread; store overnight in refrigerator. Drizzle Eggnog Icing over bread. Makes 2 loaves.

**Eggnog Icing**
Stir together ⅔ cup powdered sugar and 2–3 teaspoons canned or dairy eggnog to make an icing of drizzling consistency.

# ELEGANT *Toffee*

*Try coating this luscious toffee on both sides with milk chocolate, then dipping into ground walnuts.*

1 cup unblanched whole almonds

1 cup butter (may be half margarine)

1 cup sugar

½ teaspoon vanilla

¼ teaspoon salt

1 12-ounce package real milk chocolate pieces

½ lb. walnuts (2 generous cups), finely ground

On a foil-lined baking sheet arrange the almonds in a single layer over an area measuring 12" × 7"; set aside.

In a heavy 2-quart saucepan combine butter, sugar, vanilla, and salt. Cook over high heat, stirring constantly with a clean, dry wooden spoon until butter is melted. Continue cooking and stirring for 5–7 minutes or until candy is the color of unblanched almonds. Immediately pour candy over almonds, covering all nuts. Cool completely.

Meanwhile, in the top part of a double-boiler, melt chocolate over hot (not boiling) water. (Or, melt chocolate in a heavy saucepan over low heat, or in a microwave oven in a 1-cup glass measure, uncovered, on 100% power [high] for 1–2 minutes or until chocolate is soft enough to stir smooth, stirring every minute.) Break toffee into large pieces. Remove top part of double boiler containing chocolate to work surface. Place ground walnuts in a large bowl near chocolate.

Using a fork, dip each piece of toffee in the melted chocolate, spreading chocolate over toffee in a thin, even layer. Scrape off excess chocolate with another fork. Using 2 other forks, coat each piece very lightly with ground walnuts. Place on foil or waxed paper to set. Break into serving-size pices. Store in a tightly covered container in the refrigerator. Makes 2 pounds or 25 pieces.

# Southern PRALINES

*Originally a French candy, these nutty brown sugar treats are now a Southern tradition for all occasions.*

2 cups packed brown sugar
¾ cup evaporated milk
2 tablespoons butter
2 cups pecan halves

In a heavy medium-sized saucepan mix the brown sugar and evaporated milk. Cook and stir the mixture over medium heat to boiling. Clip a candy thermometer to the side of the pan.

Cook and stir the candy until it reaches 234°, soft-ball stage (this should take about 10 minutes). Stir in butter and pecans. Let candy stand for 10 minutes. With a spoon, beat candy vigorously until thick but still glossy (about 3 minutes).

Very quickly drop candy by spoonfuls onto foil or waxed paper. If candy becomes too stiff, stir in a few drops hot water. Cool. Store tightly covered. Makes about 20 pralines.

## STORING PRALINES

To store pralines short-term, pack the candies in a large, flat storage container, placing sheets of waxed paper between the layers. Or, individually wrap the pralines in squares of plastic wrap.

You can also freeze pralines in airtight freezer bags or containers for up to one year. After removing the candy from the freezer, let it stand several hours to warm to room temperature before opening or removing the wrapping.

*"Here we are as in olden days,*
*Happy golden days of yore.*
*Faithful friends who are dear to us*
*Gather near to us, once more."*

# APRICOT MACADAMIA
# Nut Bark

*Tart apricots create a delightful contrast to the sweetness of this delightful nut bark.*

½ cup coarsely chopped macadamia nuts, hazelnuts (filberts), or almonds
1 pound white baking pieces, cut up, or 1 pound vanilla-flavored candy coating, cut up (3 cups)
⅓ cup finely snipped dried apricots
2 tablespoons finely snipped dried apricots

To toast nuts, spread in a single layer in a shallow baking pan. Bake in a 350° oven for 7–9 minutes or until toasted, stirring occasionally. Cool.

Meanwhile, line a baking sheet with foil; set aside.

In a heavy 2-quart saucepan heat baking pieces or candy coating over low heat, stirring constantly until melted and smooth. Remove from heat. Stir in nuts and the ⅓ cup dried apricots.

Pour mixture onto the prepared baking sheet, spreading to about a 10" circle. Sprinkle with the remaining 2 tablespoons apricots, lightly pressing into mixture. Chill about 30 minutes or until firm. (Or, if using candy coating, you can let stand at room temperature for several hours or until firm.)

When firm, use the foil to lift candy from the baking sheet; break candy into pieces. Store candy, tightly covered, in the refrigerator for up to 1 month. (Or, if using candy coating, you can store, tightly covered, at room temperature.) Makes about 1¼ pounds nut bark.

# *Fairy* DROPS

*With their buttery sweet almond taste, these yummy little cookies must have been left by a Good Fairy.*

4½ cups all-purpose flour

1 teaspoon baking soda

1 teaspoon cream of tartar

1 teaspoon salt

1 cup butter

1 cup sifted powdered sugar

1 cup granulated sugar

1 cup cooking oil

2 eggs

2 teaspoons almond extract

Colored or plain sugar (optional)

Almond Frosting (optional; see below)

Crushed candy canes (optional)

In a medium mixing bowl stir together flour, baking soda, cream of tartar, and salt; set aside.

In a large mixing bowl beat butter with an electric mixer on medium-low speed until smooth. Add powdered sugar and granulated sugar; beat on medium-high speed until fluffy. Add oil, eggs, and almond extract; beat just until combined. Gradually add dry ingredients, beating on medium speed just until combined. Cover; chill dough about 30 minutes or until needed.

To shape cookies, roll rounded teaspoonfuls of dough into balls. (The dough will be soft.) Arrange balls on ungreased cookie sheets. With the palm of your hand, the bottom of a glass, or a swirled or patterned cookie stamp, gently flatten the balls to about ¼" thickness. Sprinkle with sugar, or leave plain, if planning to frost.

Bake in a 350° oven for 10–12 minutes or until edges are light brown. Transfer to a wire rack; cool completely. If desired, frost with Almond Frosting. Also, if desired, sprinkle crushed candy cane pieces over frosting. Makes 55–60 cookies.

**To Make Ahead:** Place unfrosted cookies in a freezer container; seal, label, and freeze for up to 8 months. Frost after thawing.

**Almond Frosting**

In a small mixing bowl beat ½ cup butter with an electric mixer on medium speed until fluffy. Beat in ½ teaspoon almond extract and ½ teaspoon vanilla. Alternately add 2½–3½ cups sifted powdered sugar and 3 tablespoons light cream or milk, beating until smooth and of spreading consistency. To tint, stir in a few drops food coloring, if desired. Makes about 2 cups.

## COOKIE STORAGE

To store baked cookies, cool them completely and omit the frosting so that they won't stick together. Arrange the cookies in a single layer in an airtight container or a freezer container. Cover them with a layer of waxed paper, and then add another layer of cookies. Repeat layers of cookies and waxed paper, leaving enough air space at the top to close the container easily. Store cookies at room temperature for up to 3 days or freeze them in freezer containers for up to 8 months. Frost the cookies after thawing.

# EXQUISITE *Almond Truffles*

*A true chocolate lover's delight—creamy centers enveloped by dark chocolate.*

1 cup toasted, sliced almonds
1 pound plus 4 ounces white baking pieces
¼ cup whipping cream
¼ cup cream of coconut
2 tablespoons amaretto
18 ounces (3 cups) semisweet chocolate pieces
5 tablespoons shortening

Reserve 48 almond slices; chop remaining almonds. For filling, heat and stir 1 pound of the baking pieces, the cream, and the cream of coconut just until melted. Remove from heat. Stir in chopped almonds and amaretto. Cover; freeze 2 hours or until firm. Divide filling into 48 portions; shape each portion into a ball. Freeze 15 minutes.

Meanwhile, in a 4-cup glass measure combine chocolate pieces and 3 tablespoons of the shortening. In a large glass bowl pour very warm tap water (100°–110°) to a depth of 1". Place measure with chocolate inside large bowl. (Water should cover bottom half of the measure with chocolate.) Stir chocolate constantly with a rubber spatula until chocolate is completely melted and smooth. This takes about 20 minutes; don't rush. If water cools, remove measure with chocolate. Discard cool water; add warm water. Return measure with chocolate to bowl with water. Using a fork, dip frozen balls, one at a time, into chocolate; place on a waxed-paper-lined baking sheet.

Melt the 4 remaining ounces of white baking pieces and 2 tablespoons shortening over hot water. Spoon some of the mixture over each truffle. Top each with an almond slice. Makes 48 truffles.

## MELTING CHOCOLATE

When melting the chocolate in which you will dip the truffles, be sure not to splash any water into the chocolate. Just one drop can cause the chocolate to become thick and grainy. If water should get into the chocolate, stir in additional shortening, one teaspoon at a time, until the mixture becomes shiny and smooth.

# Recipes to Share

*Turn your homemade holiday treats into gifts that keep on giving.*

*Photocopy these recipe enclosures onto colored paper; cut out; and either roll*

*up and tie with a ribbon or fold and tuck into your gift container.*

*Now your loved ones can enjoy your thoughtful gift for years to come!*

## APRICOT MACADAMIA NUT BARK

½ cup coarsely chopped
  macadamia nuts,
  hazelnuts (filberts),
  or almonds
1 pound white baking
  pieces, cut up, or 1
  pound vanilla-flavored
  candy coating, cut up
  (3 cups)

⅓ cup finely snipped
  dried apricots
2 tablespoons finely
  snipped dried apricots

To toast nuts, spread in a single layer in a shallow baking pan. Bake in a 350° oven for 7–9 minutes or until toasted, stirring occasionally. Cool.

Meanwhile, line a baking sheet with foil; set aside.

In a heavy 2-quart saucepan heat baking pieces or candy coating over low heat, stirring constantly until melted and smooth. Remove from heat. Stir in nuts and the ⅓ cup dried apricots.

Pour mixture onto the prepared baking sheet, spreading to about a 10" circle. Sprinkle with the remaining 2 tablespoons apricots, lightly pressing into mixture. Chill about 30 minutes or until firm. (Or, if using candy coating, you can let stand at room temperature for several hours or until firm.)

When firm, use the foil to lift candy from the baking sheet; break candy into pieces. Store candy, tightly covered, in the refrigerator for up to 1 month. (Or, if using candy coating, you can store, tightly covered, at room temperature.) Makes about 1¼ pounds nut bark.

## PEAR ZUCCHINI BREAD

Nonstick spray coating
2 cups all-purpose flour
1 cup rye flour
2 teaspoons pumpkin pie
  spice
1 teaspoon baking soda
½ teaspoon baking
  powder
½ teaspoon salt
2 cups chopped, peeled
  pears or one 16-ounce
  can pear halves,
  drained and chopped

1 cup granulated sugar
1 cup packed brown sugar
1 cup finely shredded,
  unpeeled zucchini
1 cup cooking oil
3 eggs
1 tablespoon vanilla
½ cup chopped pecans

Spray two 8" x 4" x 2" loaf pans with nonstick coating; set aside.

In a medium mixing bowl combine flours, pumpkin pie spice, baking soda, baking powder, and salt.

In a large mixing bowl combine pears, sugars, zucchini, oil, eggs, and vanilla; mix well. Add flour mixture; stir just until combined. Stir in chopped nuts.

Pour batter into prepared pans. Bake in a 350° oven for 55–60 minutes or until a toothpick inserted near the center comes out clean. Cool for 10 minutes on a wire rack. Remove bread from pan; cool thoroughly on rack. Wrap in plastic wrap and store overnight before slicing. Makes 2 loaves (16 slices each).

# HOLIDAY TEA RING

4¼–4¾ cups all-purpose flour
1 package active dry yeast
1 cup milk
½ cup margarine or butter
1 cup sugar
¾ teaspoon salt
3 eggs
⅓ cup margarine or butter, melted
½ cup candied red cherries, chopped
½ cup candied green cherries, chopped
½ cup candied pineapple, chopped
½ cup chopped pecans
Rum Icing (see below)

In a large mixing bowl stir together 2 cups of the flour and the yeast.

In a medium saucepan heat the milk, the ½ cup margarine or butter, ½ cup of the sugar, and the salt until warm (120°–130°). Add the milk mixture and the eggs to the flour mixture. Beat with an electric mixer on low speed for 30 seconds, scraping the sides of the bowl. Beat on high speed for 3 minutes. Stir in as much of the remaining flour as you can.

Cover and refrigerate the dough for 6–24 hours. Stir down dough. Use 3 pans: 9" pie plates, 8" x 1½" round baking pans, or 9" x1½" round baking pans. Grease; set aside.

Divide the dough into 3 portions. On a lightly floured surface, roll 1 portion into a rectangle, about 14" x 8". Brush the rectangle of dough with one-third of the melted margarine or butter. Sprinkle rectangle with one-third of the remaining ½ cup sugar. Sprinkle with one-third of the candied cherries, the candied pineapple, and the nuts.

Roll rectangle of dough loosely, starting from a long side; pinch edges together. Shape the roll into a circle, pinching the ends together. Place the circle of dough in a prepared pie plate or in a baking pan. Using scissors, cut from the outer edge almost through to the center at 1" intervals; twist each 1" piece ½ turn to the left to form a tea ring. Repeat with the 2 remaining portions of dough to make 2 more tea rings.

Cover lightly with plastic wrap; allow the dough to rise for 6–24 hours in the refrigerator. Bake tea rings in a 375° oven for about 20 minutes or until light brown. Transfer to a wire rack. Brush tea rings with Rum Icing while hot. Serve warm or at room temperature. (To freeze, wrap the cooled tea rings in freezer wrap and seal. Store up to 3 months in the freezer. Thaw overnight at room temperature.) Makes 3 tea rings (8 servings each).

**Rum Icing:** In a mixing bowl stir together 1 cup sifted powdered sugar, ¼ teaspoon rum extract, and enough hot water (about 1-2 tablespoons) to make of icing consistency.

# ELEGANT TOFFEE

1 cup unblanched whole almonds
1 cup butter (may be half margarine)
1 cup sugar
½ teaspoon vanilla
¼ teaspoon salt
1 12-ounce package real milk chocolate pieces
½ lb. walnuts (2 generous cups), finely ground

On a foil-lined baking sheet arrange the almonds in a single layer over an area measuring 12" x 7"; set aside.

In a heavy 2-quart saucepan combine butter, sugar, vanilla, and salt. Cook over high heat, stirring constantly with a clean, dry wooden spoon until butter is melted. Continue cooking and stirring for 5–7 minutes or until candy is the color of unblanched almonds. Immediately pour over almonds, covering all nuts. Cool completely.

Meanwhile, in the top part of a double-boiler, melt chocolate over hot (not boiling) water. (Or, melt chocolate in a heavy saucepan over low heat, or in a microwave oven in a 1-cup glass measure, uncovered, on 100% power [high] for 1–2 minutes or until chocolate is soft enough to stir smooth, stirring every minute.) Break toffee into large pieces. Remove top part of double boiler containing chocolate to work surface. Place ground walnuts in a large bowl near the chocolate.

Using a fork, dip each piece of toffee in the melted chocolate, spreading chocolate over toffee in a thin, even layer. Scrape off excess chocolate with another fork. Using 2 other forks, coat each piece very lightly with ground walnuts. Place on foil or waxed paper to set. Break into serving-size pices. Store in a tightly covered container in the refrigerator. Makes 2 pounds or 25 pieces.

## FAIRY DROPS

4½ cups all-purpose flour
1 teaspoon baking soda
1 teaspoon cream of tartar
1 teaspoon salt
1 cup butter
1 cup sifted powdered sugar
1 cup granulated sugar
1 cup cooking oil
2 eggs

2 teaspoons almond
    extract
Colored or plain sugar
    (optional)
Almond Frosting
    (optional; see below)
Crushed candy canes
    (optional)

In a medium mixing bowl stir together flour, baking soda, cream of tartar, and salt; set aside.

In a large mixing bowl beat butter with an electric mixer on medium-low speed until smooth. Add powdered sugar and granulated sugar; beat on medium-high speed until fluffy. Add oil, eggs, and almond extract; beat just until combined. Gradually add dry ingredients, beating on medium speed just until combined. Cover; chill dough about 30 minutes or until needed.

To shape cookies, roll rounded teaspoonfuls of dough into balls. (The dough will be soft.) Arrange balls on ungreased cookie sheets. With the palm of your hand, the bottom of a glass, or a swirled or patterned cookie stamp, gently flatten the balls to about ¼" thickness. Sprinkle with sugar or leave plain, if planning to frost.

Bake in a 350° oven for 10–12 minutes or until edges are light brown. Transfer to a wire rack; cool completely. If desired, frost with Almond Frosting. Also, if desired, sprinkle crushed candy cane pieces over frosting. Makes 55–60 cookies.

To Make Ahead: Place unfrosted cookies in a freezer container; seal, label and freeze for up to 8 months. Frost after thawing.

**Almond Frosting:** In a small mixing bowl beat ½ cup butter with an electric mixer on medium speed until fluffy. Beat in ½ teaspoon almond extract and ½ teaspoon vanilla. Alternately add 2½–3½ cups sifted powdered sugar and 3 tablespoons light cream or milk, beating until smooth and of spreading consistency. To tint, stir in a few drops food coloring, if desired. Makes about 2 cups.

## CHERRY-CHOCOLATE DROPS

1 cup margarine or butter
¾ cup packed brown
    sugar
2 egg yolks
2 ounces semisweet
    chocolate, melted
    and cooled
1½ teaspoons finely
    shredded orange peel
1 teaspoon ground
    cinnamon

1 teaspoon vanilla
¼ teaspoon salt
2¼ cups all-purpose flour
1½–2 cups finely chopped
    pecans
2 egg whites
¾ cup cherry jelly or
    preserves

In large mixing bowl beat margarine or butter and brown sugar with an electric mixer on medium speed for 30 seconds. Add egg yolks, beating well. Blend in melted chocolate, orange peel, cinnamon, vanilla, and salt. Stir in flour.

Place pecans and egg whites in 2 separate small, shallow bowls. Slightly beat egg whites with a fork. Shape dough into 1" balls. Dip each ball into egg white; roll in pecans to coat.

Place balls, 2" apart, on lightly greased baking sheets. Using your thumb, make slight a indentation in top of each cookie. Bake in 350° oven about 12 minutes or until edges are firm. Cool cookies on a wire rack. Fill centers of cooled cookies with a small spoonful of jelly or preserves. Makes about 60 cookies.

## WESTERN PEPPER JELLY

**2 medium cooking apples**
**(such as Granny Smith**
**or Jonathan), cored**
**and coarsely chopped**
**1 medium green sweet**
**pepper, seeded and**
**coarsely chopped**
**6–8 jalapeño peppers,**
**halved**
**1½ cups cider vinegar**
**5 cups sugar**

**¼ cup water**
**½ of 6-ounce package**
**liquid fruit pectin**
**(1 foil pouch)**
**¼ cup finely chopped**
**green sweet pepper**
**¼ cup finely chopped red**
**sweet pepper**
**1 small banana pepper,**
**finely chopped**

In a 4- or 5-quart Dutch oven, combine apples, the coarsely chopped green pepper, jalapeño peppers, vinegar, sugar, and ¼ cup water. Bring to a boil; reduce heat. Boil gently, uncovered, for 10 minutes. Strain mixture through a sieve, pressing with the back of a spoon to remove all liquid (should have 4 cups). Discard pulp.

Return liquid to Dutch oven; bring to a boil. Add pectin; return to boiling. Boil hard for 1 minute, stirring constantly. Remove from heat. Stir in the finely chopped red and green sweet peppers and the banana pepper.

Pour into hot, sterilized half-pint canning jars (which have been sterilized by boiling for 10 minutes). Leave ¼" headspace. Wipe rims; adjust lids. Process in boiling-water bath for 5 minutes (start timing after water boils). Remove from water bath; cool on wire rack until set (jelly will take 2–3 days to set). Makes about 5 half-pints.

Note: Chopped pepper pieces will float to top on standing.

## EXQUISITE ALMOND TRUFFLES

**1 cup toasted, sliced**
**almonds**
**1 pound plus 4 ounces**
**white baking pieces**
**¼ cup whipping cream**

**¼ cup cream of coconut**
**2 tablespoons amaretto**
**18 ounces (3 cups) semi-**
**sweet chocolate pieces**
**5 tablespoons shortening**

Reserve 48 almond slices; chop remaining almonds. For filling, heat and stir 1 pound of the baking pieces, the cream, and the cream of coconut until just melted. Remove from heat. Stir in chopped almonds and amaretto. Cover; freeze 2 hours or until firm. Divide filling into 48 portions; shape each portion into a ball. Freeze 15 minutes.

Meanwhile, in a 4-cup glass measure combine chocolate pieces and 3 tablespoons of the shortening. In a large glass bowl pour very warm tap water (100°–110°) to a depth of 1". Place measure with chocolate inside large bowl. (Water should cover bottom half of the measure with chocolate.) Stir chocolate constantly with a rubber spatula until chocolate is completely melted and smooth. This takes about 20 minutes; don't rush. If water cools, remove measure with chocolate. Discard cool water; add warm water. Return measure with chocolate to bowl with water. Using a fork, dip frozen balls, one at a time, into chocolate; place on a waxed-paper-lined baking sheet.

Melt the 4 remaining ounces of white baking pieces and 2 tablespoons shortening over hot water. Spoon some of the mixture over each truffle. Top each with an almond slice. Makes 48 truffles.

## CHRISTMAS CUTOUTS

| | |
|---|---|
| ¾ cup butter | 2 eggs |
| 2½ cups all-purpose flour | 1 teaspoon baking powder |
| 1 cup sugar | 1 teaspoon vanilla |

Beat butter in mixing bowl with electric mixer on medium to high speed 30 seconds or until softened. Add half the flour, the sugar, eggs, baking powder, and vanilla. Beat until thoroughly combined. Beat or stir in remaining flour. Divide dough in half. Cover; chill for 1–2 hours or until easy to handle.

Roll each portion on a lightly floured surface to about ⅛" thickness. Cut into desired shapes. Place 1" apart on ungreased cookie sheet.

Bake in a 375° oven for 7–8 minutes or until edges are firm and bottoms are very lightly browned. Remove cookies and cool on a wire rack. Decorate, if desired. Makes about 8 dozen.

## EGGNOG BREAD

| | |
|---|---|
| 4¾ cups all-purpose flour | 2¾ cups canned or dairy eggnog |
| ¾ cup sugar | ½ cup cooking oil |
| 4 teaspoons baking powder | ¾ cup chopped pecans |
| ½ teaspoon salt | ¾ cup snipped dried apricots |
| ½ teaspoon ground nutmeg | Eggnog Icing (see below) |
| 2 beaten eggs | |

Stir together flour, sugar, baking powder, salt, and nutmeg in a large mixing bowl. Combine eggs, eggnog, and oil; add to the dry ingredients, stirring just until combined. Stir in chopped pecans and snipped apricots.

Turn into two greased 8" x 4" x 2" loaf pans. Bake in a 350° oven for 55–60 minutes or until a toothpick inserted near center comes out clean. (Cover with foil after 40 minutes if the bread browns too quickly.)

Cool in pan for 10 minutes. Remove bread from pan; cool on wire rack. Wrap bread; store overnight in refrigerator. Drizzle Eggnog Icing over bread. Makes 2 loaves.

**Eggnog Icing:** Stir together ⅔ cup powdered sugar and 2–3 teaspoons canned or dairy eggnog to make an icing of drizzling consistency.

## GINGERED PEAR RELISH

| | |
|---|---|
| 5 cups firm, ripe pear, peeled, cored, and diced (3 pounds) | 2 tablespoons Dijon-style mustard |
| 2½ cups chopped onion | 1 tablespoon grated ginger root |
| 2 cups chopped red sweet pepper | 1 teaspoon mustard seed |
| 1 cup cider vinegar | 1 teaspoon celery seed |
| 1 cup sugar | ½ teaspoon bottled hot pepper sauce |

Bring ingredients to boiling in a Dutch oven; reduce heat. Boil gently, uncovered, 45 minutes or until slightly thickened; stir often. Remove from heat.

Ladle into hot, clean half-pint canning jars, leaving ¼" headspace. Wipe rims; adjust lids. Process in boiling-water bath for 15 minutes (start timing after water boils). Makes 6 half-pints.

## PINEAPPLE MARMALADE

| | |
|---|---|
| 2 large oranges | 1 1¾-ounce package regular powdered fruit pectin |
| 2 large lemons | |
| 1 cup unsweetened pineapple juice | 5 cups sugar |
| 1 20-ounce can crushed pineapple (juice pack) | |

Score citrus peels into 4 lengthwise sections. Remove peels with a vegetable peeler. Cut into very thin strips. In a medium saucepan combine peels and pineapple juice. Bring to a boil. Cover and simmer 20 minutes; do not drain.

Cut white membrane off fruit. Section fruit over a bowl to catch juices. Discard seeds. Add fruits and juices to peel mixture. Simmer, covered, 10 minutes more. Add undrained pineapple.

Transfer fruit mixture to an 8-quart Dutch oven; stir in pectin. Bring to full rolling boil, stirring constantly. Stir in sugar; return to full rolling boil. Boil hard 1 minute, stirring constantly. Remove from heat; quickly skim off foam.

Ladle at once into hot, clean half-pint canning jars, leaving ¼" headspace. Wipe rims; adjust lids. Process in boiling-water bath 15 minutes (start timing after water boils). Makes 7 half-pints.

# FRUIT-FLAVORED VINEGAR

**1 cup pitted tart red cherries or blueberries**

**2 cups white wine vinegar**

In a small stainless-steel or enamel saucepan combine fruit and vinegar. Bring to a boil; reduce heat. Boil gently, uncovered, for 3 minutes. Remove from heat and cover loosely with cheesecloth; cool.

Pour mixture into a clean 1-quart jar. Cover jar tightly with a nonmetallic lid (or cover with plastic wrap and then tightly seal with a metal lid). Let stand in a cool, dark place for 2 weeks.

Line a colander with several layers of 100% cotton cheesecloth. Strain vinegar mixture through the colander and let it drain into a bowl. Discard fruit. Transfer strained vinegar to a clean 1-pint glass jar or bottle. If desired, add a few additional pieces of fresh fruit to the jar or bottle. Cover jar or bottle tightly with a nonmetallic lid (or cover with plastic wrap and then seal tightly with a metal lid). Store vinegar in a cool, dark place for up to 6 months. Makes about 1½ cups (24 tablespoon-size servings).

# SOUTHERN PRALINES

**2 cups packed brown sugar**

**¾ cup evaporated milk**

**2 tablespoons butter**

**2 cups pecan halves**

In a heavy medium-sized saucepan mix the brown sugar and evaporated milk. Cook and stir the mixture over medium heat to boiling. Clip a candy thermometer to the side of the pan.

Cook and stir the candy until it reaches 234°, soft-ball stage (this should take about 10 minutes). Stir in butter and pecans. Let candy stand for 10 minutes. With a spoon, beat candy vigorously until thick but still glossy (about 3 minutes).

Very quickly drop candy by spoonfuls onto foil or waxed paper. If candy becomes too stiff, stir in a few drops hot water. Cool. Store tightly covered. Makes about 20 pralines.

Storage Tip: To protect the candy, pack it in a large, flat storage container, placing sheets of waxed paper between the layers of candy pieces. Or, wrap candy pieces individually in small pieces of plastic wrap.

# FIERY MARINATED OLIVES

**2 3-ounce jars almond-stuffed olives, drained**

**⅓ cup salad oil**

**¼ cup water**

**3 tablespoons lime juice**

**1 tablespoon snipped cilantro**

**1 tablespoon crushed red pepper**

**1 teaspoon cumin seed**

**1 clove garlic, minced**

In a small saucepan combine all ingredients. Bring to a boil; reduce heat. Simmer, covered, 5 minutes. Remove from heat. Cool to room temperature.

Use a slotted spoon to transfer olives to jars with tight-fitting lids. Pour cooking liquid over olives in jars. Cover and chill in refrigerator 4–7 days before serving. Store in refrigerator up to 3 weeks. Makes about 2 cups.

# GOLDEN FRUIT CONSERVE

**1¾ pounds nectarines (about 5)**

**1½ pounds apricots (about 15) or 1¼ pounds peaches (about 4)**

**1 cup light raisins**

**2 tablespoons lemon juice**

**5½ cups sugar**

**1 1¾-ounce package regular powdered fruit pectin**

**½ teaspoon margarine or butter**

**1 cup sliced almonds**

Peel, pit, and coarsely chop nectarines and apricots or peaches separately; mash both fruits (should have 2¼ cups nectarine mixture and 2 cups apricot). In an 8- or 10-quart kettle or Dutch oven, combine the mashed fruit, raisins, and lemon juice. Place sugar into a bowl; set aside.

Add the pectin and margarine to the fruit mixture; bring to a full rolling boil over high heat, stirring constantly with a wooden spoon. Add sugar quickly. Return to a full rolling boil, stirring constantly. Boil hard for 1 minute, stirring constantly. Remove from heat; skim off any foam with a metal spoon. Stir in the almonds.

Ladle mixture into hot, clean half-pint canning jars, leaving ¼" headspace. Wipe rims; adjust lids. Process in boiling-water bath for 15 minutes (start timing after water boils). Makes 8 half-pints.

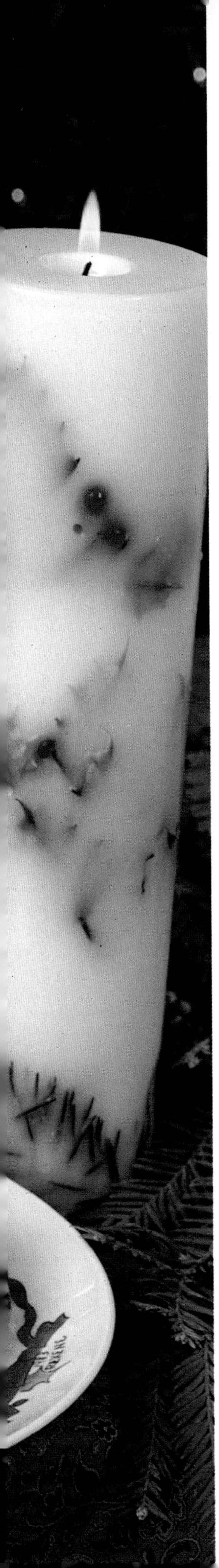

# A Holiday Feast
## FAMILY & FRIENDS TOGETHER

*Holiday meals are special times when family members gather together from all over the country to celebrate Christmas and renew their ties to each other.* ❖ *The good china and crystal are brought out of storage, silver is polished, linens are ironed, and a beautiful table is set as another way of saying "I love sharing this time with you."* ❖ *The following recipes will make savory and hearty dishes that look as wonderful as they taste and will enhance any festive occasion.*

DECEMBER CIDER
❖
QUICK TURKEY PÂTÉ
HERB DIP WITH VEGETABLES
BRIE WITH ROASTED GARLIC
MUSHROOM CAPS WITH PESTO
❖
SPINACH APPLE SALAD
❖
SMOKED SALMON PHYLLO TART
❖
GLAZED HAM
CUCUMBER BUNS
VEGETABLE TRIO
TWO-TONE POTATO CUPS
❖
PUMPKIN FLAN
CHOCOLATE-FRUIT FRANGIPANE TART
COFFEE EGGNOG

# *December* CIDER

***Warm up the holiday celebration with a mug of spiced and spiked cranberry cider, a perfect defroster after caroling and sledding.***

1 12-ounce can frozen apple juice concentrate, thawed

1 12-ounce can frozen cranberry-apple juice concentrate, thawed

6 12-ounce cans (9 cups) water

1 6-ounce can frozen lemonade concentrate, thawed

5 sticks cinnamon

1 teaspoon ground nutmeg

7 whole cloves

⅓ cup rum or cinnamon schnapps (optional)

12 sticks cinnamon (optional)

In a 4-quart Dutch oven or large kettle, combine the apple juice concentrate, cranberry-apple juice concentrate, and water. Stir in lemonade concentrate, the 5 sticks cinnamon, nutmeg, and cloves. Bring to a boil; reduce heat. Cover and simmer for 15 minutes. Remove cloves and cinnamon before serving and discard. Stir in rum or cinnamon schnapps, if desired. Pour into twelve 8-ounce mugs or glasses. Serve warm with a remaining stick of cinnamon in each mug. Makes about 3 quarts (twelve 8-ounce servings).

# *Quick* TURKEY PÂTÉ

***A food processor makes chopping and mixing this appetizer easy, but the mixture is too thick for a regular blender.***

1 pound smoked, fully cooked turkey, coarsely chopped

1 8-ounce container soft-style cream cheese with chives and onion

⅓ cup chopped celery

¼ cup milk

¼ teaspoon ground nutmeg

¼ teaspoon pepper

½ of 10-ounce package frozen chopped spinach, thawed and well drained

1 tablespoon lemon juice

¼ cup toasted, sliced almonds

Assorted crackers or flatbreads

Line a 4-cup mold with clear plastic wrap. Combine turkey, half the cream cheese, the celery, milk, nutmeg, and pepper in a food processor bowl. Cover and process until nearly smooth. Pat half of the mixture into the lined mold or pan.

Stir together spinach, lemon juice, and remaining cream cheese; layer atop the turkey mixture in pan. Place remaining turkey mixture on top. Cover and chill several hours or overnight. Unmold onto serving platter. Sprinkle with almonds. Serve with assorted crackers or flatbreads. Makes 12 servings.

*"Merry Christmas to you*
*And to you a Wassail, too.*
*And God Bless you and send you*
*a Happy New Year*
*And God send you*
*a Happy New Year."*

# *Herb Dip* WITH VEGETABLES

*Jicama slices cut into festive shapes with cookie cutters make the perfect accompaniment to this flavorful favorite.*

1 cup mayonnaise or salad dressing

¼ cup snipped parsley

¼ cup snipped chives

1 tablespoon tarragon vinegar or white wine vinegar

1 teaspoon anchovy paste or mashed drained anchovy fillets

1 clove garlic, quartered

⅛ teaspoon ground pepper

½ cup dairy sour cream

Green and red sweet pepper slices (optional)

Lettuce

Assorted vegetable dippers: green and red sweet pepper strips and jicama slices

Place half of the mayonnaise, the parsley, chives, vinegar, anchovy paste, garlic, and pepper in food processor or blender container. Cover and process or blend until smooth. Transfer to a small bowl. Stir in sour cream and remaining mayonnaise or salad dressing. Cover and chill for 2–24 hours.

To serve, transfer the dip to a serving bowl. Garnish with red and green pepper slices, if desired. Place the bowl in a lettuce-lined basket or on lettuce-lined plate. Arrange vegetables dippers around bowl. Makes about 1½ cups dip.

# *Brie* WITH ROASTED GARLIC

*When roasted, the garlic becomes mellow and
slightly sweet—a perfect blend with soft, mild brie.*

2 whole heads garlic

¼ cup olive oil or cooking oil

1 2-lb. Brie wheel or four 4½-ounce Brie wheels,
 well chilled

½ cup whole Greek olives or ripe olives, pitted and
 quartered

4 tsp. finely snipped fresh parsley

Apple wedges or warm sourdough or French bread

Place whole heads of garlic in a heavy saucepan
with olive or cooking oil. Cook, stirring, over
medium heat for 5 minutes. Cover and reduce heat
to medium-low for 15 minutes or until garlic is soft.
Remove heads of garlic from oil; drain on paper
towels; cool.

To assemble Brie, carefully slice the thin rind
off one of the flat sides of the Brie wheel(s).
Place on a baking sheet, cut side up. Divide heads
of garlic into cloves and peel. With a small, sharp
knife, slice cloves diagonally, being careful not to
completely sever each slice. Gently press garlic
cloves into fans. Arrange garlic fans and olives
atop Brie wheel(s).

Bake, uncovered, in a 400° oven for 10–12 minutes
or until brie is warm and slightly softened. Sprinkle
warm Brie with parsley. Carefully transfer to a plate
and serve with apple wedges or bread. Makes 16
servings.

# Mushroom Caps
## WITH PESTO

*Fresh basil and nuts ensure that these mushroom starters will whet everyone's appetite.*

Homemade Pesto (see below)
24–28 fresh mushrooms, 1½" in diameter
Pine nuts or walnut halves (optional)

Prepare Homemade Pesto. Remove and discard stems from mushrooms. Clean mushrooms. Spoon a rounded teaspoon of pesto into each mushroom cap. Place several pine nuts or a walnut half on top of each.

Bake in a 425° oven about 10 minutes or until hot. Drain on paper towels. Serve warm. Makes 24–28 appetizers.

**Homemade Pesto**
In a food processor bowl or blender container place ¼ cup olive oil or cooking oil, ½ cup chopped walnuts and/or pine nuts, 2 cups snipped fresh basil, ½ cup grated Parmesan cheese, and 4 cloves garlic, peeled and quartered. Process or blend until smooth. Add pepper to taste. Makes about 1 cup pesto.

# Spinach Apple SALAD

*A crisp, fresh salad is welcome at any meal, winter or summer.*

1/4 cup olive oil or salad oil
1/4 cup cider vinegar
2 teaspoons sugar
1 teaspoon finely shredded lemon peel
1/4 teaspoon salt
1/4 teaspoon pepper
2 large red apples
2–3 tablespoons lemon juice
6 cups torn spinach
2 cups shredded red cabbage
Homemade Croutons (see below)

For dressing, in a screw-top jar combine oil, vinegar, sugar, lemon peel, salt, and pepper. Cover and shake well. Chill until serving time.

For salad, slice unpeeled apple ¼" thick; brush with lemon juice. In a large bowl toss together spinach and cabbage. Shake dressing; pour over salad. Toss. Spoon onto 8 salad plates; top with apple slices and croutons. Makes 8 servings.

**Homemade Croutons**
Cut four ¾"-thick slices French bread into ¾" cubes. In a large skillet melt ¼ cup margarine or butter. Remove from heat. Stir in ⅛ teaspoon garlic powder. Add bread; stir until coated. Spread cubes in shallow pan. Bake in a 300° oven for 10 minutes. Stir. Bake 5 minutes more. Cool. Store in an airtight container. Makes 2 cups.

# *Smoked Salmon* PHYLLO TART

*Lox lovers will welcome this elegant tart combining all their favorite tastes.*

Crème Fraîche (see below)
⅓ cup margarine or butter, melted
10 sheets phyllo dough
⅛ teaspoon onion powder
⅛ teaspoon garlic salt
4 ounces smoked salmon (lox style) cut into
   ¼" strips
2 teaspoons snipped chives
¼ cup chopped toasted walnuts
Lemon-peel rose (optional)

Prepare Crème Fraîche; cover and refrigerate.

Generously brush an 11" or 12" pizza plate with some of the melted margarine or butter. Cut phyllo sheets into approximately 12" squares. Place a square of dough on the plate; brush with melted margarine. Repeat with remaining squares of phyllo and remaining melted margarine, staggering points of the dough around the edge of the plate. Fold points into pan, forming an edge.

Cut from edge to center to form 12 wedges. Bake in a 375° oven for 10–12 minutes or until golden. Cool completely. Leave on pizza plate or carefully slide off onto another serving plate, if desired. Set aside until serving time.

Stir onion powder and garlic salt into Crème Fraîche. Spread Crème Fraîche mixture evenly over phyllo crust. Arrange salmon strips on top. Sprinkle with chives and nuts. Top with lemon-peel rose, if desired. Makes 12 servings.

**Crème Fraîche**
In a small bowl stir together ½ cup dairy sour cream and ¼ cup whipping cream (do not use ultra-pasteurized cream). Cover; refrigerate 24 hours, stirring occasionally. Store in refrigerator up to 1 week. Makes ¾ cup.

## HOLIDAY DINNER PREPARATIONS

Hosting the holiday dinner can be simplified if you enlist help by asking relatives and friends to share in the menu preparations. Perhaps someone could bring homemade rolls, another could bring one of the desserts, and someone else could bring an appetizer or two to get the festivities off to a good start. That way, everyone can enjoy the special time together and no one will have to work too hard.

# *Glazed* HAM

*Drizzled with a classic orange-honey glaze, this ham is the perfect centerpiece of your holiday feast.*

1 2–2½-pound lower-sodium fully cooked
  boneless ham
¼ cup orange juice
2 tablespoons honey
1 tablespoon prepared mustard
¼ cup chicken broth
2 teaspoons cornstarch
⅓ cup orange marmalade

Make diagonal cuts about ¼" deep and 1" apart on the top of ham. Place ham on rack in shallow baking pan. Insert a meat thermometer in center of thickest portion of meat. Bake, uncovered, in a 325° oven 1½–2 hours or until meat thermometer registers 140°.

Meanwhile, combine 2 tablespoons of the orange juice, the honey, and mustard. Bring to a boil; remove from heat. After ham has baked about 1¼ hours, brush with half the glaze.

Mix remaining orange juice, the chicken broth, and cornstarch. Stir into remaining glaze. Cook and stir until thickened and bubbly. Cook and stir 2 minutes more. Stir in marmalade; heat through. Pass with sliced ham. Makes 8–10 servings.

# *Cucumber* BUNS

*Their fresh garden taste makes these buns a palate-tickling addition to your table.*

3½–3¾ cups all-purpose flour
1 package active dry yeast
2 tablespoons snipped fresh chives or 1 tablespoon
  dried chives
1 teaspoon snipped fresh dill or ½ teaspoon dried
  dillweed
1 medium cucumber, peeled and cut up (1½ cups)
½ cup dairy sour cream
¼ cup water
1 tablespoon sugar
1 teaspoon salt

In a large mixing bowl combine 1¼ cups of the flour with the yeast, chives, and dill.

In a food processor bowl, process cucumber until smooth (should have ¾ cup). In a saucepan heat and stir cucumber puree, sour cream, water, sugar, and salt until warm (120° to 130°). (Mixture will look curdled.) Add to flour mixture. Beat with an electric mixer on low to medium speed for 30 seconds, scraping bowl. Beat on high speed for 3 minutes. Using a spoon, stir in as much of the remaining flour as you can.

Turn out onto a lightly floured surface. Knead in enough of the remaining flour to make a moderately stiff dough that is smooth and elastic (6–8 minutes total). Shape into a ball. Place in a lightly greased bowl; turn once. Cover; let rise until double (about 45 minutes). Punch down dough. Turn out onto a lightly floured surface. Cover; let rest for 10 minutes. Divide into 12 pieces; shape each into a ball. Arrange in a greased 13" × 9" × 2 " baking pan, allowing space between each ball. Cover; let rise in a warm place until nearly double (about 30 minutes). Bake in a 350° oven for 20–25 minutes or until light brown. Serve warm or cool. Makes 12 rolls.

# Vegetable TRIO

*If it is easier, cook the brussels sprouts and corn on the stove top according to package directions instead of in the microwave.*

1 8-ounce package frozen brussels sprouts
1 8-ounce package frozen baby corn on the cob
2 tablespoons water
3 tablespoons brown sugar
3 tablespoons margarine or butter
1 teaspoon vinegar
1 large onion, thinly sliced and separated into rings

In a 2-quart microwave-safe casserole, combine brussels sprouts, corn, and water. Micro-cook, covered, on 100% power (high) for 8 to 10 minutes or until vegetables are just crisp-tender, stirring once. Drain.

Meanwhile, in a large saucepan combine brown sugar, margarine or butter, and vinegar. Cook and stir over medium heat for 1–2 minutes or until blended. Add onions. Cook, uncovered, over low heat for 10–12 minutes or until onions are glazed and tender, stirring occasionally. Add corn mixture and stir to coat. Cook for 1–2 minutes more to heat through. Makes 8 servings.

*"Follow me in merry measure*
*Fa la la  la la la  la la la,*
*While I sing of Yuletide pleasure*
*Fa la la la la  la la la la"*

---

## HOW TO
## Keep Holiday Eating Lighter

❖ **To help slim down holiday cooking, why not give these suggestions a try:**

Grease pans with nonstick spray coating and/or use pans with nonstick coating.

Skim fat from soups and gravies.

Trim fat from poultry and meats before cooking.

Bake the poultry stuffing separately in a casserole to keep the bread from soaking up fatty turkey drippings.

Use lower-fat dairy products, except in cookie baking.

Cut back on the amount of meat used in some recipes and extend it with vegetables. And select leaner cuts of meat.

Choose lower-sodium processed food products if you want to reduce the amount of sodium in your diet.

Substitute 2 egg whites for 1 whole egg in many recipes to cut cholesterol.

❖ **To avoid holiday overeating, how about these ideas:**

Curb your hunger at a holiday party by eating a nutritious snack before you leave home. That way you'll eat less of the party-rich foods.

Take tiny portions of rich foods and load up on fresh fruits and vegetables.

Skip seconds when passed and/or avoid a second trip through the buffet line.

# Two-Tone POTATO CUPS

*A colorful blend of sweet potatoes and white potatoes show off in this elegant side dish. After the ham is finished baking, remove it from the oven, cover, and keep warm. Increase oven temperature to 500° to brown the potatoes.*

6 medium red-skinned potatoes (2 pounds), cooked and drained

4 medium sweet potatoes (2 pounds), cooked and drained

¼ cup margarine or butter

2 egg whites

½ teaspoon onion powder

2 egg yolks

¼ cup margarine or butter, melted

Peel all of the potatoes. In 2 separate mixing bowls mash the white potatoes and the sweet potatoes with an electric mixer on low speed until smooth, adding 2 tablespoons of the margarine or butter to each. Beat egg whites and onion powder into white potatoes. Beat egg yolks into sweet potatoes. Season both potato mixtures with salt and white pepper to taste.

Line a baking sheet with foil; spray with nonstick spray coating. Using a wooden spoon, spread about ¼ cup of the sweet potato mixture into a 2½- to 3" nest on the foil. Repeat with the rest of the sweet potato mixture, making 16 nests total.

Spoon the white potato mixture into a pastry bag fitted with a decorative tip. Pipe the white potato mixture into the center of the sweet potato nests. Loosely cover nests with plastic wrap and chill for 2–24 hours.

At serving time, drizzle the melted margarine or butter over the potato nests. Bake the nests, uncovered, in a 500° oven for 10–12 minutes or until golden. (Or, broil potato nests 4" from heat about 7 minutes). Let stand for 1–2 minutes. Use a wide spatula to carefully transfer the nests to dinner plates. Makes 8 servings.

# Pumpkin FLAN

*This luscious custard dessert tastes like a crustless pumpkin pie with caramel sauce.*

1½ cup sugar

4 beaten eggs

1 6-ounce can pumpkin

1 2-ounce can evaporated milk

1 teaspoon ground cinnamon

1 teaspoon vanilla

½ teaspoon ground ginger

½ teaspoon ground nutmeg

¼ teaspoon salt

Sweetened whipped cream (optional)

Ground nutmeg (optional)

In a large heavy skillet cook 1 cup of the sugar over medium-high heat until sugar begins to melt; do not stir, just shake skillet occasionally. When sugar starts to melt, reduce heat to low; cook, stirring frequently, until sugar is golden brown. Quickly pour sugar into a 10" deep pie plate or a 10" quiche dish. Tilt to evenly coat bottom. Place pie plate or quiche dish into a large roasting pan. Place on rack in oven.

In a large mixing bowl stir together the eggs, pumpkin, milk, remaining ½ cup sugar, cinnamon, vanilla, ginger, nutmeg, and salt. Pour pumpkin mixture atop sugar in pie plate or quiche dish. Pour boiling water into roasting pan around pie plate or quiche dish to a depth of ½". Bake in a 350° oven for 50–55 minutes for pie plate or 45–50 minutes for quiche dish, or until a knife inserted near center comes out clean. Cool. Chill, covered, for 4–24 hours.

To serve, loosen edges of flan with a knife, slipping point of knife down sides of flan to let air in. Invert flan onto a serving platter. Top with sweetened whipped cream and nutmeg if desired. Makes 10 servings.

# CHOCOLATE-FRUIT
# *Frangipane* TART

*Rich with almond, chocolate, and fruit flavors, this
distinctive tart is the perfect end to any holiday meal.*

Frangipane Tart Pastry (see below)

1 8-ounce package semisweet chocolate

½ cup water

1 8-ounce can almond paste

¾ cup sugar

¾ cup butter

5 eggs

1 cup sifted cake flour or ¾ cup plus 2 tablespoons
    sifted all-purpose flour

⅓ cup apricot preserves

1 tablespoon water

1 16-ounce can pear halves, drained

1 8¾-ounce can unpeeled apricot halves, drained and
    sliced

½ cup fresh raspberries

Toasted sliced almonds (optional)

Whipped cream (optional)

Prepare Frangipane Tart Pastry. On a lightly
floured surface, flatten chilled dough with hands.
Roll dough from center to edges, forming a 12"
circle. Loosely wrap around rolling pin. Unroll onto
an ungreased 10" fluted quiche pan or springform
pan with a removable bottom. Ease into pan, being
careful not to stretch pastry. Trim pastry even with
rim of quiche pan or 1½" up sides of springform pan.
Set aside.

For filling, in a saucepan melt chocolate with
½ cup water over low heat, stirring constantly. Cool.

In a medium mixing bowl combine almond paste
and sugar; beat with an electric mixer on medium
speed until crumbly. Add butter; beat until very
creamy. Add eggs, 1 at a time, beating until combined. Add flour; beat on low speed just until
combined. Add chocolate mixture; beat on low
speed just until combined.

Pour filling into prepared pastry. Place on a baking
sheet. Bake in a 350° oven for 1¼ hours or until
toothpick inserted near center comes out clean.
Cool in pan on a wire rack. Cover and chill until
serving.

For topping, in a saucepan combine apricot preserves
and the remaining 1 tablespoon water; heat and
stir until melted. If desired, strain through a
sieve.

Place pear halves, flat side down, on a cutting
board. Cutting from wide end to narrow end,
slice pears lengthwise into ¼" thick slices, leaving
attached at the narrow end.

Remove tart from pan. Arrange fanned pear
halves and apricot slices on top, starting at the
outside edge. Place raspberries in the center.
Spoon preserves over fruit. Before serving, top
with almonds, if desired. Serve with whipped
cream, if desired. Makes 16 servings.

**Frangipane Tart Pastry**

In a large mixing bowl beat ⅔ cup butter with an
electric mixer on medium speed until softened.
Add ⅔ cup sugar; beat until light and fluffy. Beat
in 2 egg yolks. Add 2 cups sifted cake flour or 1¾
cups sifted all-purpose flour. Add ¼ teaspoon
baking powder; beat until combined. Wrap dough
in plastic wrap; chill until firm enough to roll.

# COFFEE *Eggnog*

*Use refrigerated, canned, or homemade eggnog for this creamy, rich treat.*

1 tablespoon hot water

1½ teaspoon instant coffee crystals

4 cups dairy or canned eggnog

2 tablespoons brown sugar

⅛ teaspoon ground cinnamon

¼ cup coffee liqueur (optional)

¼ cup brandy or bourbon (optional)

½ cup whipping cream

¼ cup sifted powdered sugar

½ teaspoon vanilla

In a large mixing bowl combine hot water and the 1¼ teaspoons coffee crystals; stir to dissolve. Add eggnog, brown sugar, and cinnamon. Beat with a rotary mixer or whisk until sugar is dissolved. Stir in coffee liqueur and brandy or bourbon. Chill thoroughly. At serving time, in a small mixing bowl beat whipping cream, powdered sugar, and vanilla with an electric mixer on high speed until soft peaks form. Pour eggnog mixture into 4-ounce cups or glasses; top with whipped cream and sprinkle with additional coffee crystals. Makes 8–10 (4-ounce) servings.

# HOW TO
# *Garnish with Citrus*

One of the great challenges of any holiday dinner lies in making your table reflect the special nature of the gathering. Family and friends around a holiday feast deserve more than the standard parsley and paprika touches.

Try some of these easy, new presentation ideas to make your special Christmas foods look just as wonderful as they taste.

Citrus fruits have alway been a welcome part of the holiday celebration: Oranges and grapefruits have wreathed many a Southern doorway, and generations of children have delighted to find sweet, sunny oranges in their Christmas stockings.

You can make these simple citrus trims with lemons, oranges, or limes. Or you can combine citrus fruits for colorful effects.

**Double Citrus Twists:** Cut ⅛-inch-thick citrus slices. Make a cut from the center to the outside edge of each slice. Stack two slices and twist the cut ends in opposite directions. For color contrast, use a lemon and lime slice.

**Orange Rose:** Cut a long, thin strip of orange peel. Roll up the strip to form a coil or rose shape, using your fingers for shaping. If desired, garnish with mint leaves and several orange peel strips for the center of the flower.

**Lemon Slice Curl:** Cut a lemon slice from the center to the outside edge, then overlap edges. Dollop sour cream or mayonnaise in the center and garnish with a small parsley sprig.

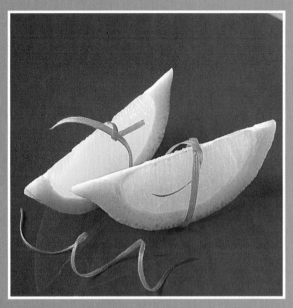

**Lemon Wedges:** Cut lemon into wedges and tie with a long chive or narrow strip of green onion.

**Notched Slices:** Cut six to eight vertical strips from a lemon, lime, or orange before slicing. Use lemon zester for easier cutting.

**Citrus Strips:** Use a vegetable peeler to cut the peel off oranges, lemons, and/or limes. Scrape off the white membrane. Use a sharp knife to cut peel into strips and tie into knots (see several ways in photo) or bows.

# Sources

The project directions in this book call for materials that are widely available in craft stores. If you have difficulty locating specific items, contact the manufacturers or distributors listed below to find sources in your area.

Binny & Smith
Consumer Information
1100 Church Lane
P.O. Box 431
Easton, PA 18044
(800) 272-9652
Acrylic paints, air-drying modeling compound

C.M. Offray & Son, Inc.
Route 24, Box 601
Chester, NJ 07930-0601
Ribbons

Charles Craft, Inc.
P.O. Box 1049
Laurinburg, NC 28353
(800) 346-4721 or
(910) 276-4721
Even-weave fabric for cross-stitch

Chase Products Company
19th Street and Gardner Road
Broadview, IL 60153
(800) 323-7136
Spray glitter

Decart, Inc.
P.O. Box 309
Morrisville, VT 05661
(802) 888-4217
Makers of DEKA-Gloss

DMC Corporation
10 Port Kearny Building
South Kearny, NJ 07032-4688
(201) 589-0606
Embroidery floss

Designs by Bentwood, Inc.
170 Big Star Drive
P.O. Box 1676
Thomasville, GA 31792
(912) 226-1223
Sewing box: Medium-size Oval Tine

Endar Corporation
Florasense
28780 Single Oak Drive
Temecula, CA
(800) 562-9974
Christmas potpourri

Flora-Lite Company
P.O. Box 4119
Clearwater,FL 34618
(813) 443-0369
Battery-operated miniature strings of Christmas lights

Herr's & Acclaim
70 Eastgate Drive
Danville, IL 61832
(217) 442-4121
30-gauge sheets of tin and copper; aluminum, brass, and copper foil

Hill Design, Inc.
Brown Bag Cookie Art
77 Regional Drive
Concord, NH 03301
(603) 226-1984
Clay cookie molds

Keypoint Company, Inc.
1343 Round Table Drive
Dallas, TX 75247
(800) 521-5004 or
(214) 630-3544
Mushroom birds; nests; natural birdhouses

Madeira Marketing, Ltd.
600 East 9th Street
Michigan City, IN 46360
Rainbow Glissen Gloss
(800) 275-9004
Metallic threads for cross-stitch

Matthew Thomas Designs
4235 Arden Way
San Diego, CA 92103
(619) 565-2638
Blank canvas stockings

Pres-On Merchandising Corp.
Dept. BH
1020 South Westgate Drive
Addison, IL 60101
(800) 323-1745
Self-stick mounting boards; bell frame in Cross-Stitch Bells

Stik 'N' Puffs
available through:
Banar Designs
P.O. Box 483
Fallbrook, CA 92088
(619) 728-0344
Self-adhesive stuffed heart shapes

Tender Heart Treasures, Ltd.
10525 "J" Street
Omaha, NE 68127
(800) 443-1367
Wire hearts candle ring

Texas Baskets
P.O. Box 1110
Jacksonville, TX 75766
(800) 657-2200 or
(903) 586-8014
Diamond-weave handled baskets

Woodworks
4500 Anderson Boulevard
Fort Worth, TX 76117
(800) 722-0311 or
(817) 281-4447
Wood shapes; spools; snowman candlesticks; apple birdhouses

Zweigart Fabrics
for order information, contact:
Needleworker's Delight
100 Claridge Place
Colonia, NJ 07067
(800) 931-4545 or
(980) 388-4545
Even-weave fabric; needlepoint canvas

# Acknowledgments

**DECK THE HALLS**
*Designers*

Country Copper and Tin, 10
*Dave Risney*

Glimmery Angel, 12
*Dave Risney*

Card Caddy, 14
*Joni Prittie*

Seed Bead Heart, 15
*Arin Duggins*

Mini Stocking, 16
*Ren Vasilev*

Christmas Quilt, 18
*Joni Prittie*

Teddy Bear Tree Skirt, 21
*Jodee Risney*

Teddy Angel Stocking, 22
*Jodee Risney*

Ribbon Weave Stocking, 25
*Jodee Risney*

Homespun Wreaths, 26
*Linda Glover*

Jingle Bell, 27
*Linda Glover*

Cross-Stitch Bells, 28
*Bright Star*

Cross-Stitch Snowflakes, 32
*Linda Glover*

Cross-Stitch Kringle, 34
*Linda Dawn*

Father Christmas, 36
*Linda Schreiber*

**NATURAL WONDERS**
*Designers*

Hearty Elf, 44
*Joni Prittie*

A Trinket Wreath, 45
*Joni Prittie*

Apple Birdhouse, 46
*Joni Prittie*

Hearts and Flowers, 47
*Joni Prittie*

Cardinal Garland, 48
*Linda Dawn*

Winter Basket, 50
*Naturally Yours*

Candle Ring, 53
*Joni Prittie*

Pretty Pouches, 53
*Jodee Risney*

Potpourri Wreath, 54
*Linda Dawn*

Poinsettia Wreath, 55
*Joni Prittie*

Della Robbia Garland, 56
*Joni Prittie*

**CRAFTED WITH LOVE**
*Designers*

Memento Frames, 60
*Jodee Risney*

Fish Frame, 60
*Dave Risney*

Patchwork Frame, 63
*Linda Glover*

Treasure Keeper, 64
*Joni Prittie*

Thimble Set, 67
*Joni Prittie*

Sewing Box, 67
*Joni Prittie*

Patchwork Pincushion, 68
*Linda Glover*

For Her Lapel, 69
*Jodee Risney*

Seed Bead Pendant, 70
*Arin Duggins*

Seed Bead Earrings, 71
*Arin Duggins*

For Specs and Keys, 72
*Ren Vasilev*

Holiday Sachets, 75
*Joni Prittie*

Light-Up Cap, 78
*Dave Risney, II*

Set for Winter, 79
*Jodee Risney*

Pine Tree Tea Set, 81
*Joni Prittie*

Rocking Cow, 82
*Joni Prittie*

Cinnamon Bear, 82
*Joni Prittie*

Mini Christmas Tree, 83
*Jodee Risney*

Teddy Bear Tea Party, 85
*Joni Prittie*

Tortoise Shell Boxes, 86
*Joni Prittie*

Candlestick Snowmen, 86
*Joni Prittie*

**FAMILY FUN**
*Designers*

Star-Power Elves, 95
*Joni Prittie*

Pompon Wreath, 95
*Joni Prittie*

Candy-Mold Ornaments, 97
*Joni Prittie*

Glitter-Berry Stocking, 97
*Joni Prittie*

Spool Tree, 99
*Joni Prittie*

Spool Dolly, 100
*Linda Glover*

Gingerbread Angels, 103
*Joni Prittie*

Gingerbread Boys on
the Run, 104
*Joni Prittie*

# Index

"And so I'm offering this simple wish
To kids from one to ninety-two.
Although it's been said many times,
many ways,
      Merry Christmas to you."